Globalization, Consumer Culture and Identity

Globalization, Consumer Culture and Identity

The Middle Class in a Postmodern Society

Antony Palackal

RAWAT PUBLICATIONS

Jaipur • New Delhi • Bangalore • Hyderabad • Guwahati

ISBN 81-316-0396-2

Published by
Prem Rawat for **Rawat Publications**
Satyam Apts, Sector 3, Jawahar Nagar, Jaipur 302 004 (India)
Phone: 0141 265 1748 / 7006 Fax: 0141 265 1748
E-mail: info@rawatbooks.com
Website: www.rawatbooks.com

New Delhi Office
4858/24, Ansari Road, Daryaganj, New Delhi 110 002
Phone: 011 2326 3290

Also at *Bangalore, Hyderabad* and *Guwahati*

Typeset by Rawat Computers, Jaipur
Printed at Chaman Enterprises, New Delhi

Dedicated to

THE JESUIT SOCIETY

which sharpened and sustained my concerns about consumer culture and reinforced my orientation to simplicity in life.

Contents

Preface

The origin of this book has the history of a chequered journey of personal search and reflection over a decade. From the time I was initiated into systematic sociological gaze and imagination, I was disturbingly struck by the growing desire in individuals for conspicuous consumption without being very sensitive to the plight of the *neighbour* who is struggling to *sustain* for want of bare necessities in life. I was soon to realize that it was nothing but the chaotic manifestations of the gradual, but relentless shift of the latter stage of modernity from a *society of producers* to a *society of consumers* in the wake of the post-liberal currents engulfing the globe. The difference that this passage brings forth is so deep and ubiquitous that makes our society a separate and distinct kind – a consumer society. In a society of consumers, the masses are re-cast as *flawed consumers* and *being poor* today appears to draw its meaning primarily from the plight of a flawed consumer. It becomes quite different to be poor in a society of consumers, wherein life-projects are built around consumer choices rather than work, skills or jobs.

My doctoral dissertation was an attempt to unravel this emerging phenomenon of consumer culture with its far-reaching socio-political and cultural implications. The category of consumption then became the primary subject of my analysis. Later, the question of identity that entails one's freedom in making decisions and choices in life in the locus of consumer culture, became a more important field of investigation for me. Does consumption characterize the mode of being, a way of gaining identity, meaning and prestige in a globalized society – was the cardinal question that reverberated in me that gradually took the shape of this book. The central issue that the book attempts to address is the manner in which the overarching ideology of consumption has been instrumental in reworking individual's identity through narratives about consumption and materiality in a post-liberal world.

The fruition of the book, therefore, is closely linked to my own personal journey in orienting and setting priorities and making choices in life. This biographical element of the book is reflected in its treatment as an ethnographic narrative emphasizing qualitative methods. But for the ambience of the Jesuit Society wherein I cherished my being and movement during this phase of the journey, I would not have oriented my sociological gaze in this direction. Hence, with profound sense of indebtedness, I dedicate this book to the Jesuit Society which enabled me to substantively pitch my world view and approach to societal realities that partly culminated in this work.

My deep sentiments of gratitude are due to Prof. Jacob John Kattakayam, currently the President of Indian Sociological Society, who accompanied me in this academic pursuit with sustaining interest, support and appreciation as a mentor and guide. The circle of friends and benefactors, near and far who enveloped me with affection and encouragement in my staggering moments in the making of this book – I dare not list their names, but gracefully place on record, my unending sentiments of gratefulness to all of them. However, the first place should go to Ansu, my wife whose gentle and caring but amazingly strengthening presence made this book truly possible. Her critical reading of the manuscript has enriched the book substantially. I also owe sincere thanks to Rawat Publications for publishing this work.

Thiruvananthapuram **Antony Palackal**
23 April 2010

List of Figures

List of Tables

Glossary

Vanitha	–	'lady', a popular women's fortnightly in Malayalam
Mahilaratnam	–	'woman gem', a Malayalam popular periodical for women
Grahalakshmi	–	'home prosperity', popular periodical in Malayalam for women
Malayala Manorama	–	a popular weekly in Malayalam
Azhchappathippu Sthrijanmam	–	'woman's life', a Malayalam Tele-serial
kadakeni	–	debt trap
blade	–	a colloquial usage as a metaphor denoting exorbitant interests for the loan money collected mostly on a daily basis from the debtors as being cut with a sharp blade
panayam	–	getting loan from financiers on gold security
ayalkoottams	–	neighbourhood groups
videshi	–	pertaining to foreign as against the native
pettikkada	–	street-side vending shop

swadhesi	–	pertaining to something native and indigenous
thattu kada	–	food and snack sheds on the way side, open especially at night
pottu	–	popularly known as *bindi*, pattern of colourful mark girls wear on the forehead
kesalankara malsaram	–	hair style competition
adi poli	–	a recent vernacular and popular expression for something very exciting and interesting
Nadodumbum Naduve Odanam	–	a colloquial proverb meaning swim along with the current
jatis	–	castes and subcastes

CHAPTER 1

Identity Revisited

Vignette

Maya received quality education in her schooling and is a postgraduate in Social Work. Her father was a businessman, and her mother, a teacher. She worked as a community organizer at first and later as a counsellor for a long time in several establishments. At present, she is working as a counsellor in a reputed organization in Thiruvananthapuram – the capital of Kerala state. She is 35-year plus; her husband is an engineer and her son, a middle school student. She originally hailed from a rural setting in Mavelikkara, not very far from Thiruvananthapuram, in the northern direction. She moved to Thiruvananthapuram after her marriage in 1996. One day Maya talked to me about the new shopping culture and the manner in which the changed nature of the market creates an atmosphere in which people tend to be caught up by the tentacles of the new market culture unaware:

> Our buying habit has undergone substantial changes these days. Earlier, we used to prepare the list of necessary items in advance, and made it a point to purchase only those items in the list. However, now, the situation is quite different, especially with the advent of super markets so common amidst us. When we walk into the departmental store with a basket and are free to pick and choose any item that we want, the

> tendency is to pick simply whatever items capture our attention. Sometimes we would not have even thought of getting those items. Since they are found there, we feel like getting them just for the sake of tasting or using them once. Like this we get lots of foodstuffs and snacks, especially those in the packets. We may not really need them, but still we just want to try them. And, the interesting part of it is that some of them are really useless and go as sheer waste. Then, we regret saying, "Oh! We have simply wasted money." I have particularly experienced this with stuffs meant to make soft drinks.

Maya points to the contemporary market situation in which aspirations of the people are whetted by the increasing exposure to the kind of life that tends to replicate the consumer propensities of the West. What appears to set people apart will be what they buy rather than what they are. Their identities are defined mainly by their taste in clothes, food, appearance and lifestyle. This academic expedition has been embarked upon with the specific question whether consumption characterizes the mode of being, a way of gaining identity, meaning and prestige in contemporary society, with special reference to the middle class. This is meant to examine whether possession of objects and display of signs of affluence affect the subjective view of the middle class. This exploration necessitates looking into the perceivable shifts in the cognitive and emotive experiences of body and appearance in the lives of the middle class with special reference to women and young people. Therefore, an attempt has been made here to conduct an empirical enquiry into the practices of everyday life and also to discover how subjects mediate the processes constructing identities in the emerging context ushered in by globalization.

The advent of globalization in the Indian subcontinent has brought the ever-widening middle class into new prominence in terms of its ability to consume. The middle class, as the predominant social group in the Indian society, has been engaged in forms of consumption that resembled the cosmopolitan cultural forms in other parts of the world. This sociological gaze intends to explore the manner in which consumer culture constructs the identity of the middle class people. The cardinal question that the book addresses is "how does consumer culture constitute middle class in a globalized society?"

Annie works as the chief of a well-established centre of Voluntary Coordinating Agency for Adoption. She has three children. The eldest boy is in the high school and the younger one in the primary. The only daughter is just three years old. During one of my conversations, Annie touched on this important dimension of the widespread buying habit of the people of modern days. She said, "People buy too much these days. ... Actually, it is a status affair. If certain items are missing in our home, it will affect our image. That is the reason why people even go to the extreme extent of availing loans in order to get those prestigious items." Samir, a postgraduate student, corroborating this opinion on the perceived changes in the market scenario and the buying habit, says:

> Newer items struck us everyday that we are tempted to possess them; or the attitude is that if I don't buy those items and my neighbours or friends buy, it is bad for my status. I may be thrown out of that group or I may get excommunicated. I have noticed this tendency in our group; if somebody buys a shirt, I too should have that; if somebody gets a bike, I too should acquire that model, that sort of tendency.

The perceptions of Annie and Samir point to the fact that the increased buying habit of the people today will have to be looked at relative to consumers' notions of the variables that go in the making of status and image in the orbit of consumer culture. Consumer culture, the pervasive by-product of globalization, forms the specific canvas of the book. Cultural underpinnings of globalization, spearheaded by the permeating consumer culture, impinge on the formation of the self and the issue of identity is more pressing and contested than ever before in contemporary societies. The field of consumer culture, it is argued, is the privileged stage where the contestations and negotiations of identities occur in contemporary society.

Contemporary phenomenon of globalization constitutes the larger context of the book. The objective social process of globalization (macro), driven primarily by the global economy and communication and information technology, inheres simultaneously a subjective component (micro) that is reflected in the small and concrete, the spatially particular, the self and the cultural symbols – all of which bear the signature of the global. Based on this argument, the book broadly seeks to deal with the sociological debate regarding the dialectics between the macro and the micro aspects of globalization, which is reflected in the paradoxical relation between *global* and *local*. More specifically, the book proposes to embark upon a sociological inquiry into the everyday practices of social life in the age of globalization that unravels the subjective orientations in building trajectories of life.

Chequered Terrain

Opinion on the consequences of globalization is sharply divided, especially with respect to cultural changes. Some hold euphoric expectations of global prosperity, while others view this process pessimistically as the cause of many social evils. A thoroughly progressive and liberating phenomenon helps to explore the potential for greater human connectedness and the spread of human rights, democracy, health care and improved intercultural understanding worldwide. Conversely, it is widely attacked as heralding in a new and voracious phase of Western capitalism and the imposition of Americanized culture (in the form of television, videos, pop music, films and advertisement and other Western goods) on vulnerable communities, which are unable to protect themselves from the sheer volume and intensity of foreign imports.[1] The talk is of electronic imperialism with the overloaded flow of media from America as the world's superpower and the growing disparity between the world's (technology-owning) 'information rich' and 'information poor'.[2]

What is undeniable is that globalization, in one form or other, has its impact on the lives of everyone on the planet, irrespective of their age, class, ethnicity, gender or wherever they live. Craik (1994) has observed that it is changing consciousness, too, as everyone from everywhere becomes more globally aware and oriented. In this sense, globalization might justifiably be claimed as the defining feature of human society at the start of the twenty-first century. Hence, globalization is not incidental to our lives today. It is a shift in our very life circumstances and chances; it has come to be the way we now live.

Globalization as a social process has spearheaded a 'world of culture in motion' generating newer spaces of political and cultural economies. It is a world where cultural subjects and objects, in individuals and significant forms (such as capital, commodities, desires, dreams, images and signs), have become unhinged from particular localities, as it were, eroding the 'natural' connection or isomorphism between culture and locale. The book seeks to dwell on this central issue of global-local relations and opens up an investigation on the nature and dynamics of the cultural flows across the globalized world. Underlying this issue of 'global-local dialectics' is the question of cultural homogeneity versus heterogeneity. The cultural homogeneity thesis boils down to a fear that every place is, at least culturally, becoming similar and those local and national cultures get drowned in a shallow and synthetic global culture. The volume is set in the background of this global apprehension and so it intends to look at the idea that if the world is a mosaic of cultures, then what are the alternative perspectives on the shapes and boundaries of cultures?

Hence, this sociological reflection primarily seeks to dwell on the dialectics between the 'global' and the 'local'. So, the articulation of the global and the local with the ways in which globalizing processes exist in the context of, and must come to terms with, the realities of particular societies, with their accumulated cultures and ways of life. It is, therefore, preoccupied with the experiences of people living in specific localities when everyday life appears to be more and more contingent on globally extensive social processes. It intends to embark upon an examination of the practices of everyday life and tries to discover how subjects mediate the processes of globalization. Globalization, it is observed, incorporates a dual identity of 'the global in the local' and 'the local in the global'. The enquiry on the local response to global integration will hopefully enable us to look at this basic variant of globalization as to the nature of local embeddedness in the global. Hence, the study also deals with the question whether our world is moving towards cultural homogenization or heterogenization.

The experience of globalization becomes tangible when its effect is perceived locally, preferably, at the micro level. The continued reorganization of market conditions and market networks affects the livelihood of people and their life trajectories. This becomes clearer when one begins to look at the changing patterns of consumption and the manner in which they relate persons and communities to the global market. At the local level, it is difficult to understand the subtle ramifications of the global market and its dynamics as it is being played out in the everyday destiny of an ordinary person in relation to his/her locality.

The book opens up a line of enquiry on the local consequences of this global interconnectedness, i.e., the effects of the operations of globalization at the micro level. The constituent component of this enquiry involves the analysis of the global spread of market culture with its consumer goods and styles. It consists of a sociological gaze into the manner in which people appropriate/indigenise or negotiate/resist the consumption of these goods and styles, and the contingencies they bring forth in the local culture. In the larger canvas, it seeks to dwell on the contemporary cultural processes and the perceived changes vis-à-vis the current wave of globalization.

Consumption – A Way of Life

'Consumption' has become a fundamental modality in a globalized world. Globalization, as an economic and socio-cultural process, has taken a more pervasive form, leading to an increasing similarity of production and consumption patterns and a worldwide movement of products, people, services and cultures. The forces of the market and the rules of the status battle of life are inescapable in today's consumer world. Consumption has become associated with the present so much that members of a society often consider modern goods as necessities indispensable for life today. Goods that were out of the reach of local people earlier have come to be seen as essential requirements to live a satisfied life. Consumption as an activity has become a modality of today's globalized life.

Consumption emerges as a definition of identities both at the individual and collective levels, more than anything else. In the present-day market culture, it appears that our identity is moulded as consumers; consumer goods are seen as a privileged part of identity. In the contemporary market culture, liberty, in practice, boils down to consumer's choice. To understand the nature and dynamics of the local consequences of global interconnectedness, it becomes imperative to make a sociological gaze on consumption – the most pervasive subjective realm of experience of the individuals and collectivities in their everyday life.

In recent years, Indians are engaged in forms of consumption that resemble the cosmopolitan cultural forms in other parts of the world (Kemper, 1993; Appadurai, 1996b). The ever-growing proliferation of consumer goods and commodities of all kinds in myriad forms and nature that are flowing into the local markets, the most vibrant and dynamic marketing and delivery systems in abundance, the dynamism of the food and restaurant industries, the growing national frenzy over sports (such as cricket), the palpable growth in domestic tourism, the rapid inroads made by television and video cassettes, CDs and DVDs into the domain of the cinema, the penetration of the countryside by voracious media and advertising forces, and the general commodification of cultural objects are all part of this process which has many other expressions as well.

Since the eighties, the Government of India gradually abandoned the earlier state perspective that was led by an ideal of self-reliance. When the state opted for a liberalized policy entailing free imports, less restrictions and encouragement to foreign investors, then the lifting of controls on production resulted in a considerable increase in the availability of consumer goods in the Indian market. As a result, radical changes occurred in the consumption behaviour of Indians in general. Simultaneously, there has been a fast spread of exposure to commercial television. Nowadays, numerous television channels bring to Indian homes images of luxurious lifestyles that encourage unscrupulous consumption. Wessel (2001), in her ethnographic study on the Indian community in Baroda (now Vadodara), has made an interesting observation that consumption has come to be associated so much with the present that the members of the middle class often see modern goods as necessities indispensable for their lives today. Prior to the advent of the consumption era, life was simple. The range of available goods present in the lives of earlier generations was limited, and their desires were in tune with that reality. Now, the presence of wealth and a wider array of goods have paved the way for a new standard in consumptive aspirations.

Identity – A Problematic

In the arena of consumer culture, the issue of 'identity' has come to surface as more pressing and contested than ever before in contemporary societies. Against all collective identities, individuals are attempting to construct their own personal identities, which often are, however, highly mediated by collective forces. The quest for individuality and particularity in one's look, image, style and life continues apace – both at the individual and collective levels. In reflexive modernization thesis, Giddens (1991) postulated a sharp decline in the power and legitimacy of authoritative norms of the yesteryears. Instead of the normative fabric of the recent past, there occurred a corresponding trend in exploring new forms of identity and a subsequent decline in the capacity of social institutions (such as religion, family, educational portals etc.) to reflect in people's biographies. Although these changes represent a kind of 'freeing' of individuals from the constraints of institutions and normative standards, they also make people much more susceptible to the risks of the vital decisions of their lives, notably in the market.

Interestingly, as a result of the commercial lifestyle, transnational and trans-cultural clusters of aspirations tend to define people's existence much more than what they really are. This defining identity-kit has come to stay as more 'real' to people today than the surviving vestiges of class solidarity. Indeed, the two great traditional markers of collective identity, nation and class, are seen to be disintegrating under the onslaught of global media. Media market nowadays has the power to move people not just to buy the products of the cultural industries, but to buy into networks that offer forms of community/collective identities that can transcend the confines of class, gender, regional and national alliances.

Our identity seems to be moulded as consumers. Consumer goods are considered as a privileged part of identity. It is something we could call consumer identity. Consumption is very likely to be the mode of being, a way of gaining identity, meaning and prestige in the contemporary society (Sarup, 1996). Generally, in the contemporary market culture, liberty boils down to consumer choice. 'Life politics' has been perceived now-a-days as politics of decisions to be made amidst an array of choices in and through the dialectical tension of freedom and constraint (Giddens, 1991). In a globalized world, the individual is faced with a bulk of information deriving from a diversity of mediated experiences. This turbulent cultural context throws multifaceted tensions and difficulties in the development of the self. First and foremost, the myriads of problems affect the formation of the personal identity itself. One needs to watch television only for a short period to realize the enormous emphasis placed on physical appearance.

Undoubtedly, contemporary social milieu brings to surface the potent issue of identity as a crucial problem that requires serious sociological gaze. The dynamics of the interplay between consumer culture and construction of identities needs to be explored. An examination of the manner in which people's identities take shape in the engulfing sphere of consumer culture, would throw light on the socio-cultural changes taking place at the local level. At the centre of this question of identity are the issues, such as who or what, influence and define the identity of individuals, social groups, nations and cultures in the globalized scenario of the contemporary society. The cardinal questions are: (1) Does this new market culture that globalization has ushered in alter individuals' and groups' sense of themselves? (2) Are there new forms of subjectivity, and, if so, what are their effects on personal and social identity? This is as much cultural as an intellectual formulation because it involves a study on the practice and experience of globalism in its micro-manifestations.

This crucial issue of the construction of identity in contemporary society may be pursued through a conceptual framework of "resistance to and accommodation of" the consumer culture so as to outline the contours of strategies involved in the formation of personal and collective identities. That is to say, unravel the elements of negotiation, ambiguities, reconciliation, and assimilation and revolt involved in constructing identities in the face of the innumerable consumer goods and services. A sociological enquiry of this kind is of paramount importance as it illumines the dynamics of the current global-local interconnections that is well expressed in the phraseology: "everything everywhere, yet everywhere different."

Media studies have brought to light the fact that identity in a globalized society is basically a construct. For instance, it can be constantly changed, refined and fine-tuned. Above all, identity is a question of image, style and looks of an individual. Kellner (1995) has raised the question whether 'identity' is treated primarily as a modern or postmodern issue; linking it with the current debate on modernity and postmodernity. It is equally arbitrary and open to debate as to whether one posits that we are in a situation of late modernity or postmodernity. The larger canvas of this problematic issue includes whether postmodern identity could be read either as intensification of features already present in modernity, or as a new configuration with new emphasis that one could describe as postmodern?

Middle Class – New Historic Bloc

In India, discourses on nationalism from the outset have been closely linked to the categories of class and nation. Anti-colonial nationalism is characterized as a fundamentally middle class phenomenon. Postcolonial nationalism has also been embedded in the discourse of the middle class. Hence, it is not surprising that the dominant vision of the future of the Indian nation is fundamentally middle class in its orientation. Even less surprising is the fact that the Doordarshan officials, policy makers, serial producers and advertisers have conceptualized the expanding middle class as their 'target audience'. No wonder that the middle class phenomenon in India has become a subject of domestic debate and international attention since the mid–1980s. The international attention followed the sudden recognition that the rising Indian middle class would be a major market in the 1990s.

In 1991, when India embarked on a process of economic reforms, opening up its economy and inviting foreign investment,[3] the Indian middle class secured new status. *Business India* reported: "When liberalization began in 1991, the Indian middle class acquired a new prominence as one of the world's largest markets, as a different breed of entrepreneurs and consumers"[4] (August 18, 2002, pp. 52–58). A new magazine, whose glossy pages promised to provide an 'authoritative guide to good living,' came up with the following proposition:

> The economic liberalization that has been sweeping across the country for the last few years has altered the lives of a large section of India's burgeoning middle class. They have become far more international in their outlook and aspirations, more sophisticated and liberal in lifestyle and attitudes, and certainly more adventurous and demanding in terms of holiday and leisure activities. One of the psychological legacies of the Nehruvian socialistic era was that the more affluent sections of society were branded as being rather vulgar, and spending money to live well was considered an ever-greater sin. Today, that stigma seems to have vanished from many. "*With the new Manmohanomics, there are many more opportunities to make money and even more avenues to spend it*" (Arun Purie, in the inaugural issue of *India Today Plus*, First Quarter).

When state controls on production were lifted and India opened the door to foreign investors, it results a considerable increase in the availability of consumer goods in the Indian market. Simultaneously, there has been a fast spread of exposure to commercial television. Numerous television channels embarked on bringing Indian homes the images of luxurious lifestyles that emphasized consumption. The availability of the new consumer goods, combined with the exposure to satellite television, has contributed to changes in the lifestyle among all strata of society. Historically, this constituted the momentous period that marked the emergence of middle class as an outstanding section; so was the emergence of this class as a significant group in the Indian polity.

Several scholars have pointed out the difficulties of delineating the sociological boundaries of middle class (Tanter and Young, 1990). The middle class in general is a heterogeneous historical bloc with differential access to relations of production, status and political power. What constituted them as middle class was their aspiration to upward mobility and modernity through consumerism. It has been correctly noted that the new economic policies enabled the people of middle class to consume goods that had till recently were considered as luxury items but were now perceived as crucial indices of upward mobility – household appliances, toiletries, packaged foods and other consumer goods (Mankekar, 1999). In this way, the demographic expansion of the middle class was reinforced by its cultural constitution.

Since the early nineties, when liberalization policies became more pronounced, the middle class has become the focus of considerable media attention. This middle class, an elastic group ranging from 100 to 350 million depending on the criteria employed, suddenly became an entity worthy of observation and debate that focussed on their ability to consume.[5] The middle class has been targeted as the prime consumers of the new goods that liberalization policies had made available in the Indian market. Hence, the 'liberalization' package, tailored to make India a player in the 'globalized' economy, suddenly directed the spotlight on the middle class for an entirely new reason: If India was to open up to the world markets, it was essential to know how much it could buy. It became evident that the middle class contained the largest concentration of purchasing power in India today, although there is much debate about its actual size,[6] consumption patterns and the pace of its growth in the years to come. Varma (1998) asserts:

> The logic of economic reform, therefore, dictated that the middle class now be analysed not for its lack of ideological moorings, or its lack of commitment to anything but its own material well-being, or for its utter insensitivity to social and

> moral causes, *but for its craving for and ability to buy what the developed countries could sell to it*. ... In this process the size of the Indian middle class became, for the first time, a matter of crucial importance. ... Overnight the consumerist thirst of the middle class became an asset, a sign of the dynamism of the Indian market. ... Its numbers have grown and so has its purchasing power, and ever more strikingly, its consumerist ambitions (pp. 170–173).

Socio-political developments in India in recent years have often been articulated in terms of crisis (Kothari, 1989; Kohli, 1991; Baxi and Parekh, 1995; Saberwal, 1996). It is pointed out that the middle class, having been engulfed by consumer culture, is in the grip of a moral crisis; and this moral crisis is closely tied with abandoning the Gandhian ideal of self-reliance and a commitment to a form of development that includes the poor and the disadvantaged. Solidarity with the poor, the authors explained, is incompatible with the present middle class orientation towards personal economic success and consumption. This upliftment in the value system of the middle class and the resultant cultural transformation of the Indian society also need to be examined.

Women and Youth

Market operations in consumer culture target women as a separate category. The world of advertisements, fashion, beauty, cosmetics and health care privilege women and their body vis-à-vis the commercial ends of the market (Gupta, 2000). Hence, the scope and space of women as a category in this emerging market culture need to be delineated. A closer look at the experience of womanhood and the construction of femininity and feminine aesthetics in relation to the commercial ends and demands of the global market constitutes an important task of this study. In the background of the prevailing feminist discourses on identity assertions and actions of resistance and resurgence, this sociological gaze intends to open up a line of inquiry on the effects of consumer operations on the feminine predicament.

It has been argued that female literacy was a key factor in the high levels of literacy that Kerala achieved (Gulati, 1992;

Ramachandran, 1996). Literacy in general and female literacy in particular, was an essential facilitator of Kerala's achievements in the spheres of health and demographic change. Undoubtedly, there is a substantial difference in respect of the attitude and treatment of women in Kerala compared to the rest of the country; it is also well evidenced in the sex ratio of the state that is tilted towards women. Actually, there exists a different gender culture in Kerala, which is unique to the Indian subcontinent. In this favourably gendered climate of Kerala and the consequences of globalization on middle class women, the formation of their identity as a special domain of enquiry is significant.

It is the youth as a group who grew up along with the current trends of globalization. Contemporary studies on youth culture have often portrayed their culture as constructions and expressions of identity that draw on young people's experiences of assimilation and resistance to consumer culture and its ethos (Willis, 1977; Hebdige, 1979; Cohen, 1994). The young in the middle class are even more susceptible to imitating the West than their parents were. For instance, regarding the Miss World contest in Bangalore in 1996, Varma (1998) observed that young, Westernised middle class Indians just could not understand what the bigoted 'obscurantists' were protesting about. In the same way, those who have opposed it could not comprehend how a section of Indians could so enthusiastically welcome a western '*tamasha*' which insulted Indian culture by allowing foreign women to parade themselves half-naked on Indian soil.

Young people tend to claim specific space for their own. Styles and outfits are important aspects of identity for boys and girls, especially when they are adolescents. They are in touch with and at the same time preoccupied with the emerging trends of the globalized world in comparison with their elders. The stress of youthfulness should also be reckoned with. Youth becomes a stereotype not only for commercial success, but also for sexual attraction that has become a constituent ingredient to commercial success. Needless to say, more and more young people are attracted towards the seductive domain of commercial advertisements and simulations of the contemporary global market culture. In short, young people are exposed in an esteemed fashion to the details of the globalized world and to its consumer culture. As a group they move and have their being in the enticing field of consumer culture and its value system. An ethnographic gaze focused on the younger generation as a category, in comparison with that of their older generation, it is hoped, will bring out clearly the ramifications of the cultural consequences of globalization on Kerala.

Location

Kerala, the southernmost state of India, constitutes the specific context in which this sociological reflection is taken on. The state of Kerala is widely acclaimed for its unique pattern of development. The 'Kerala model' of development has become a much-debated topic all over the world and it has been regarded as a model for many other developing societies. The state, with its distinctive socio-economic and demographic characteristics, has been compared with developed nations[7] (Ramachandran, 1996; Oommen, 1992, 1999, Vol. 1 and 2). Despite its enviable progress and unique features, Kerala remains one of the poorer regions among the states in India. The bleak economic scenario of the state contradicts its well-publicized achievements in recent years. The per capita income, for instance, is notably below the national average and that of many other states (George, 1993). Paradoxical, as it were, a high level of consumption marks the living standard of the people. Kerala has been referred to as a consumerist society.

Not surprisingly, the middle class forms a significant and outstanding group in Kerala. In recent years, the middle class people of Kerala have been engaged in forms of consumption that resemble the cosmopolitan cultural forms of the more developed regions of the world. For instance, Krishna Kumar (1994) observes:

> As you drive from Thiruvananthapuram towards Ernakulam (two districts in the State lying at a distance of around 250 kms) and beyond, you are struck by the emergent character of Kerala's new middle class. Palatial houses, mosques that rise out of the horizon in the shocking splendour of fresh chemical paints and hotels waiting for customers are no simple symbolic artifacts (p. 346).

It is assumed that a closer ethnographic gaze into the consumption patterns, styles and modalities of the people of Kerala will be a key to the gamut of issues related to the construction of identities and the associated questions of cultural changes in India today. The main contention built along the course of this sociological query is that the consumer world is the privileged platform where contestations and negotiations of identities occur in the present-day society. This book, therefore, intends to focus on the issue: Is the present-day identity of the middle class most importantly marked by what they consume? This is closely connected to the earlier formulation of the cardinal question that is expected to guide this academic endeavour: How does consumer culture constitute Malayalis? Hence, the book embarks upon an academic expedition into the dynamics of the formation of identities of middle class people in the emerging context of consumer culture with special reference to the state of Kerala. The dimensions of this task involve the following:

1. Outline the global factors that affect the choices of consumer goods of the middle class today.
2. Trace the relation between consumer culture and identity in a globalizing society.
3. Identify the elements of accommodation and resistance to consumer culture in the purview of globalization, in the making of identities of middle class.
4. Find out the elements that constitute identity in the middle class in the age of globalization.
5. Examine the specific ways in which consumer culture influences the construction of identity of the middle class.

This reflexive journey has been undertaken bearing in mind the basic belief that the contemporary consumer world substantially influences the construction of identities at the personal and collective levels. Aspects of this belief include the following assumptions that guide us in this sociological endeavour:

1. Consumer behaviour is the privileged entry point to gauge the influence of contemporary globalization in its effect on the everyday lives of the middle class.

2. The middle class as a social group is highly prone to the impact of consumer culture.
3. Global means of communication and information on consumer culture greatly contribute to the choices of consumer items, particularly of the middle class.
4. Contemporary globalization with its characteristic element of consumer culture influences the identity construction of the middle class.
5. There are more elements of accommodation of the global consumer culture than elements of resistance in the everyday lives of the middle class.
6. Youth, as a category, is highly vulnerable to the influence of contemporary consumer culture.
7. Notions of middle class women on their physical appearance and body are primarily defined by the prevailing consumer culture.

Method

At the substratum of this sociological project that explores the cultural ambiguities and negotiations of a society in the construction of identities, lies culture and its change. This endeavour is guided by the idea that the present-day culture is marked by an experience of cultural transformation and fragmentation in the social gamut of consumer culture that characterizes current wave of globalization. Thus, an anthropological detour has been deployed to produce ethnography of the cultural effects of globalization. This phenomenological approach towards data gathering was employed in order to gather insights from the insiders' perspective.

In order to construct this ethnography, I moved with a group of respondents falling within the selected category of middle class under this academic scrutiny. I have developed friendly acquaintances with all of them and have been closely associating with them as a colleague or teacher. I have subjected their consumer behaviour and lifestyle to an ordered and systematic observation engaging in frequent conversations with them with the aid of a semi-structured interview guide. The purpose of this ethnographic query was to understand how participants perceive the world around them and consequently how their world views get shaped and conditioned as they encountered global economy with its new market culture. My ethnographic engagement in this phase focused on respondents' perceptions and interpretations of social processes within the context of their everyday interactions and choices.

This ethnographic endeavour has enabled me to gather data on everyday perceptions, aspirations, attitudes, and value systems of the participants who were identified as middle class men and women. The data of the qualitative nature has been presented in the form of narratives and case stories so as to form ethnography of the making of identities of the middle class in this part of the globe in the age of globalization. The phenomenological preoccupation with this ethnographic gaze was to render primacy to gather insights from probing and understanding the 'insiders'. All the participants in this ethnographic project belonged to Thiruvananthapuram district because the pilot study that I had administered prior to this ethnographic project, revealed to me the fact that Thiruvananthapuram, being the capital of the state of Kerala, contained a cross-section of the middle class from every corner of the state. Later, my sample for the quantitative data represented participants from eleven districts out of fourteen of the state, besides those who originally belonged to Thiruvananthapuram.

This qualitative data was further substantiated with the content analysis of a selected print and visual popular media of the region with a view to throw more light on the most tangible ramifications of consumer culture as it is being played out in the everyday lives of the middle class community in Kerala. The qualitative data gathered through the ethnographic project and the content analysis of popular media was supported and corroborated by a set of quantitative data gathered through the use of a closed-ended questionnaire. The questionnaire was administered on a sample of 360 respondents in Thiruvananthapuram. An individual belonging to a middle class household was treated as the unit of the sample. The middle class, as a category, has been delimited to two characteristic features: (1) those endowed with a gainful employment in the non-agricultural areas of occupation; and (2) whose employment fetches a certain amount of regular and secure income. Considering the nature of the occupation, the respondents were classified as (1) salaried, (2) business, and (3) foreign migrant.

Another important preoccupation at this phase of quantitative data gathering was with regard to the division of the respondents based on their income. This was resolved by taking the monthly salary of the lowest category employee, say Class IV, in a government service, which is ordinarily considered as a middle class in Kerala. The monthly income of a Class IV government employee was fixed as the bottom level income of the middle class which amounted to Rs 4,500–5,000 according to the present pay scales in Kerala. Accordingly, the middle class was further classified on the basis of the income variation as lower-middle class, middle class and upper-middle class within the limits of a monthly income ranging from Rs 5,000–10,000, Rs 10,000–15,000 and Rs 15,000–20,000, respectively.

Profile

The sample was grouped into three age groups: (1) 15–30, (2) 31–55, and (3) 56–70. The age group 15–30 was comprised of the youth. After thirty years of age, individuals normally shift to another phase of their life mostly as married and employed persons. This phase of the individuals will be substantially different from its earlier phase characterized as youthhood and marked by significant changes in the tastes and behaviour as a consumer. This stage, which is commonly known as adulthood, normally comes to close by the time when people reach their fifties. In Kerala, the age for retirement is 55, which is also fixed for all the private establishments except government and university sectors. Therefore, the second category in the study was determined as those individuals of the sample belonging to the age group of 31–55. After fifties and particularly after retirement, again a shift in the choices and priorities in the consumer behaviour of the individuals may be perceived. Hence, the third category of the sample was fixed as those individuals of the sample beyond the age of 56. Seventy was the upper age limit of the sample. The mean age of the sample is 33.22 with a standard deviation of 12.61.

The age-wise distribution of the sample reveals that the maximum number of the respondents belonged to the category of youth. However, the mean age is slightly above this age group. This seems to have only further enriched the study, as the general behaviour and attitudes regarding the various aspects of the issue under investigation will not totally be coloured and conditioned by the dominant category – the youth of the sample. This mean age, therefore, in a sense, informs us that the views expressed are representational and falls mainly within the category of 'adults' in terms of life cycle.

The participants of the study were comprised of 223 males (61.9%) and 137 females (38.1%). As mentioned earlier, the middle class that comprised the specific target group of the study has been classified into three categories, viz., lower-middle (Rs 5,000–10,000), middle-middle (Rs 10,000–15,000) and upper-middle (Rs 15,000–20,000), based on the amount of income per month. The sample consisted of 53.9 per cent lower-middle income category that constituted the highest group of respondents and 32.5 per cent of middle-middle income group with 117 respondents. The lowest number of respondents belonged to the third income group of upper-middle with 13.6 per cent.

A district-wise analysis of the sample revealed the fact that the respondents were fairly representative of a cross-section of Kerala. Although majority of them hailed from Thiruvananthapuram – the capital district itself, where the study has been administered – a sizeable proportion contributing to more than one-fourth of the sample (26.7%) belonged to other parts of Kerala spreading over eleven districts. The respondents were mainly from three major religions in Kerala, viz., Hindus, Muslims and Christians. The maximum number of respondents (58.3%) belonged to the Hindu religion, which is the religious majority in Kerala. Christians formed the second highest category (33.3%), and the sample contained only 29 (8.1%) respondents from the Muslim community. One participant did not profess faith in any religion. The caste-wise distribution of the respondents showed that the general category formed the highest group with 214 participants (59.4%), followed by members belonging to OBCs (Other Backward Classes) contributing to 129 (35.8%) persons, while Scheduled Caste (SC) groups consisted of 16, i.e., constituting 4.4 per cent of the total sample.

Majority of the respondents had degree level education (33.3%) and at the other end of the spectrum comprised of the group of respondents who obtained PhD consisting of 1.7 per cent of the sample. The school-educated category of respondents formed 10.3 per cent with 37 respondents and the technically educated was less than this category comprising 9.2 per cent (33 persons) of the sample. Both of these categories together constituted only 19.5 per cent. This means that the educational qualification of the rest of the sample, i.e., 80.5 per cent of the respondents or 290 respondents, was pre-degree or above.

On the basis of occupation respondents were classified as (1) those working, (2) not working, and (3) studying in order to distinguish themselves from those working and those studying. However, the majority of the respondents consisting 58.6 per cent belonged to the 'working' category and the 'studying' category comprised of 92 respondents (26%) and so about half the number of the respondents belonged to the 'working' group. Approximately 25.6 per cent of the respondents did not engage themselves in any occupation.

The working group of the sample was further categorized into 'salaried,' 'business' and 'foreign.' This classification was made in order to know the basis of income of the family of each respondent. The result showed that 51.1 per cent of respondents (184 persons) belonged to the salaried class, whereas 7.8 per cent and 1.4 per cent of respondents had business and foreign remittance respectively as their primary means of income. However, 39.7 per cent belonged to the fourth category of occupation, i.e., those having various other occupations that fetched rather regular income to the household.

Task Ahead

As stated earlier, in the contemporary market culture, liberty boils down to consumer choice. Hence, the ways in which people use, dominate or are dominated and related to objects constitutes an important area of study. The dimensions of this sociological exercise address the following questions:

1. Does consumption characterize the mode of being, a way of gaining identity, meaning and prestige of the middle class people in a society like Kerala?
2. How does possession of objects and display of signs of affluence affect their subjective view?
3. To what extent do simulations, new forms of technology, culture and experience constitute the postmodern era when it comes to the everyday lives of the middle class in general, and its womenfolk and youth in particular?
4. Are the new developments in mass media altering the sense of the middle class?
5. Does the mass media, television for instance, privatise individuals, trapping them in a universe of simulacra in which it is impossible to distinguish between the spectacle and the real, and in consequence diminish social sensitivity?
6. What are the perceivable shifts in the cognitive and emotive experience of body and appearance in the lives of the middle class with special reference to women and young people?

In view of the avowed task of this sociological enterprise, the book is conceived in two sections with seven chapters. The first section with two chapters (chapters 2 and 3) is primarily designed as conceptual and theoretical. The second chapter attempts to elaborate the cardinal concepts that the book intends to dwell on, mainly, consumer culture and identity vis-à-vis the debates on postmodernity. The third chapter strives for a discussion on the appropriate conceptual and theoretical propositions which are found useful in understanding and explaining the issues under consideration.

The second section is empirical which is spreading over five chapters. This section is designed as a narrative that constitutes ethnography of the micro-level effects of globalization. Chapter 4 makes an attempt to elaborate the factors, which affect the choices of the consumers in a global market culture. This enquiry is taken forward in the next chapter (chapter 5) that tries to explicate the role and impact of the visual media along with advertisements in mirroring consumer culture and thereby impinge the choices of middle class as the prime consumers. Chapter 6 seeks to examine the nature and dynamics of accommodation and resistance in operation when different segments of the middle class encounter consumer culture. Chapter 7 intends to dwell on the specific ways in which the middle class appropriates and negotiates their identity in the domain of consumer culture and seeks to delineate the parameters of identity in a post-capitalistic regime. The concluding chapter tries to carve out the vicissitudes of indigenous culture that is subjected to a process of decomposition and finds its values in transition in the wake of the engulfing consumer culture.

In the final analysis, this academic project at a deeper level is located in the contemporary debate on culture and cultural change in the wake of contemporary globalization. The understanding of the significance of globalization in the cultural making and remaking of a society becomes important in this knowledge-building process. At the base of this enquiry lies the idea that addresses one and the same fundamental question in the sociological parlance on cultural change: is the world a mosaic of cultures or not? What are the alternative perspectives on the shapes and boundaries of cultures that can we come up with in the study of globalization and consumer culture in relation to local cultures? This investigation ultimately, it is hoped, will throw newer insights into the dynamics of 'global flows' and 'cultural closure'.

Notes

1. For example, an important aspect of globalization is that many non-Western economies are hugely dependent on the making of Western goods for the Western market: 40 per cent of Levi's jeans (one of the great symbols of America) are manufactured in Tunisia, 30 per cent in Turkey, and 30 per cent in UK. In terms of the global fashion industry, countries like Taiwan, Bangladesh, South Korea, Hong Kong and China have become mass producers of clothes for the West (Craik, 1994).
2. Commenting on the findings of the UN's latest Human Development Report, that the total wealth of the top 358 'global billionaires' equals

the combined incomes of 2.3 billion poorest people (45% of the world's population). Victor Keegan called the present reshuffling of the world resources 'a new form of highway robbery'. Indeed, only 22 per cent of global wealth belongs to the so-called 'developing countries,' which account for about 80 per cent of the world population. And yet, this is by no means the limit the present polarization is likely to reach, since the share of the global income currently apportioned to the poor is still smaller: in 1991, 85 per cent of the world's population received only 15 per cent of its income (Bauman, 1998, pp. 70–71).

3. In mid-1991, the then Prime Minister, Narasimha Rao, guided by the Finance Minister, Dr Manmohan Singh, announced a series of economic reforms, which were expected to help dismantle some of the inefficient state controls on the Indian economy and facilitate its greater integration with the world economy.
4. See also 'The Great Indian Middle Class' by Debashish Mukherji in *The Week*, Anniversary Issue, December 30, 2001.
5. See, *Far Eastern Economic Review*, January 14, 1993, February 2, 1995, March 17, 1994; *India Today*, April 15, 1995; *Business Today*, issue 4, 1996; *Fortune*, issue 5, 1997.
6. Several systematic surveys were carried out to gauge their numbers; for instance, on the one extreme end is the recent estimate of 300 million (58 million households) of NCAER based on survey of the expenditure in rural and urban households between 1986 and 1990. At the other end is the estimate of 35–40 million based on income tax assets, individual holders of company shares, ownership of durable consumer goods, ownership of houses in urban areas and executive level employment in the organized sector (quoted in Varma, 1998, p. 171). Refer also to Fakih, S. N. "Size of Middle Class Estimates and Implications" in *Financial Express*, Delhi, February 2, 1987, p. 5.
7. To mention a few unique features of Kerala: the state has the highest number of literates in the country, both men and women; the sex ratio is in favour of women; contrary to the common all India trend, Kerala's population growth rate declined considerably; Kerala has the lowest birth rate and death rate in the country; infant mortality rate too is the lowest which is comparable with that of Washington; fertility is one of the least rates recorded – less than two per couple; so is the maternal mortality rate: two for 1000 deliveries, in sharp contrast to forty-five for India; life expectancy of the people of Kerala at birth is well above the all India average; the average morbidity rate too is an all-time low (Ramachandran, 1996).

CHAPTER 2

Consumer Culture

Economic globalization constitutes the core of the current process of globalization, though global trade networks have always been a part of the modern world. But, the recent wave of economic globalization is fundamentally different from its earlier manifestations. It is the unprecedented intensification and acceleration of the open flow of communication and movement of people, capital, technologies, goods, images and knowledge beyond national borders. As a result, although it is against the international trade networks of the past, there operates a global marketplace, which binds producers and consumers across the world through a chain of commodity exchanges. The global labour force is also dispersed along the production links of these commodity chains (McMichael, 1996).

Economic policies in India have undergone mammoth change during the last two decades and more changes are in the process of being implemented. The end of 1991 witnessed the reforms of liberalization and the consequent structural changes. It involved drastic changes in the economic policies, consisting of liberalization of trade, deregulation of governmental restrictions, encouragement of private initiative and so on. These developments are multifaceted. They involve interlocking economic, ecological, sociocultural and political activities that penetrate all areas of everyday life. As Dreze and Sen (2002) rightly points out, "the reforms that were introduced by the end of 1991 have concentrated mainly on removing the 'licence raj' and the 'ever-proliferating bureaucracy'. The liberalization programme has led to a considerable expansion of exports in some sectors and a substantial improvement in the foreign exchange balance. It has also called attention to a vibrant international response involving renewed interest in the possibilities of the Indian economy".[1] The outcome of these newly introduced liberalization policies and the structural adjustment programmes in the Indian economic sphere was so perceptible that three years after the reforms began, the *Forbes* magazine even pictured India on its cover page (23 May 1994), with the declaration: "India may be the best emerging market of all." As a result of this globalized market, radically there developed new forms and ways of life in India centred on consumption. This cultural scenario is referred to as consumer culture.

Consumption Centric

Consumer culture essentially characterizes and manifests the contemporary wave of globalization. It is an all-embracing mode of consumption and lifestyle along with the accompanied codes of values, attitudes and ethics. Hence, consumer culture broadly refers to the pervading atmosphere that encompasses the entire gamut of material as well as symbolic goods and items available to the public for consumption. This wide spectrum of consumer culture includes all types of consumable goods and items of various brands and varieties of expensive non-essential food and nutritional products; all sorts of health care and medical drugs, devices and techniques; a whole gamut of cosmetics and ornaments; various kinds of costly home appliances, electrical gadgets and other paraphernalia; a variety of brands and models of clothing and footwear; the galaxy of modern automobiles, vehicles and means of transportation; the proliferating real estate business, housing projects, mansions, hotels and related accessories; tourism and travel industry and business; the unprecedented galaxy of modes of communication and information, including that of cyber space; the print, audio and visual channels of entertainment; the spectacles of sports and games, fashion, beauty etc.; the different forms, ways and means of their advertisement and display for their publicity and promotion; and various forms of signs, images, symbols and representations available to humans today. The pervading atmosphere of the world view, attitudes, ethos, values and behaviour generated specifically on account of these consumable goods and items may be viewed as constituting the domain of consumer culture.

Improved modes of communication and information, together with rationalizations in methods of distribution (e.g., inventory control, packaging and market feedback), have made it possible for commodities to move around through the market system at a faster pace; twenty-four-hour-a-day financial services and markets have increased the mobility of capital; and the mobilization of fashion in niche markets has facilitated a speed-up in the pace of consumption in clothing, ornaments and across a wide range of recreational activities and life-styles such as pop music styles, leisure and sporting habits and video and children's games (Inda and Rosaldo, 2002).

The Anthropology of Globalization: A Reader, edited by Jonathan Xavier Inda and Renato Rosaldo (2002), offers an anthropological perspective on globalization. It presents an ethnographic chapter by Meyer. The narrative of this chapter succinctly depicts the effect of the global flow of consumer goods on the locals of Ghana, who profess a particular belief system. Meyer shows how Pentacostalist churches in Ghana play an important role in defining the cultural significance of one important aspect of 'global flow' – goods spread through the market. The churches present these goods as dangerous to the integrity of the person, for their alleged association with the devil and spirits who are the devil's agents. The Pentacostalist church "presents itself as the sole instance which is truly able to help people handle globalization" (2002, p. 173) and also provides people with a solution to this problem – through prayer the dangers can be neutralized. Meyer points out how the problematic aspects of consumption have largely been ignored until now, and "it looks as if the main problem which people face in the field of consumption is the unequal distribution of money to buy western commodities" (2002, p. 171). The flow of modern goods forms an attraction and a challenge simultaneously; through the Pentacostalist church, the challenge becomes neutralized.

Identity Struggle

If we track the global flow of commodities and concentrate on the consumption of goods, we find that the goods often mediate the 'encounter' between peoples and cultures around the world. Friedman (2002) explores how consumption becomes an aspect of broader cultural strategies of self-definition and self-maintenance. He suggests that strategies of consumption can only be truly grasped when we understand the specific way in which desire is constituted. He assumes that consumption is one of the important dynamic aspects of the formation of personhood or selfhood (Friedman, 2002, p. 234). He writes, "Consumption within the bounds of the world systems is always a consumption of identity, canalised by a negotiation between self-definition and the array of possibilities offered by the capitalist market" (2002, p. 235). When goods are regarded as the building blocks of life-worlds, they can be further understood as constituents of selfhood and social identity. Hence, the formation of identity encompasses the practice of consumption.

The very notion of identity has been a rather generic one in the history of Western social theory. The term 'identity' derives from the Latin root *idem* implying sameness and continuity. Discussions of identity take two major forms – psychodynamic and sociological (Marshall, ed., 1994). The central thrust of both traditions has been to challenge essentialist understandings of the concept which assume a unique core or essence to identity, the 'real me', which is coherent and remains more or less the same throughout life. Against this the emphasis within both sociological and psychoanalytic theories has been, in varying degrees, the invented and constructed character of identity.

The psychodynamic theory stresses the inner core of a psychic structure as having a continuous identity. The psychodynamic tradition emerges with Freud's theory of identification which states that the child comes to assimilate external persons or objects, generally the superego of the parent. The psycho-historian, Erik Erikson, considered identity as a process 'located' in the core of the individual and also in the core of his or her communal culture, hence, making a connection between community and individual. He developed the concept 'identity crisis' during the Second World War, with reference to patients who had "lost a sense of personal sameness and historical continuity".

The sociological tradition of the identity theory is linked to symbolic interactionism and emerges from the pragmatic theory of the 'self,' discussed by William James and George Herbert Mead (Mead, 1934/1962). The 'self' is a distinctively human capacity which enables people to reflect on their nature and the social world through communication and language. Both James and Mead considered the 'self' as a process with two phrases: the 'I', consists of the knower, inner, subjective, creative, determining and unknowable; and the 'Me', comprising more of the known, outer-determined, creative and social. Identification is a process of naming, of placing an individual in socially constructed categories, with language holding a central position. In the later works of Erving Goffman (1959) and Peter Berger (1963), 'identity' is conceived to be socially bestowed, socially sustained and socially transformed.

Developments in social theory associated with structuralism and post-structuralism share the concern with language and representation more broadly, which was integral to the symbolic interactionist approach to identity. Structuralism and post-structuralism, however, more assertively emphasize the constitutive or deeply formative role of language and representation in the making of identity (Saussure, 1966). Saussure's (1966) account of language has been used to argue that all social and cultural meanings are produced within language or systems of representation more generally. In other words, the world around us, as well as our place in it, is given meaning, made meaningful, within representation. Therefore, 'who we are', our sense of identity, is shaped by the meanings attached to particular attributes, capacities and forms of conduct.

The French philosopher, Michel Foucault (1977), building on the broad thrust of Saussure's arguments, took this account of identity further in his works on discourse and discursive formations. Foucault adds an element, which has become central to recent accounts of identity. This is the insistence that we, as individuals, inhabit multiple identities. There are two key dimensions to this assertion. The first is that different discourses generate particular and often divergent positions for agency and identity. Within this perspective, each is addressed by a range of possible versions of the self (such as devout believer, taxpayer, football supporter, or trade union member). The second dimension is that the multiple identities we inhabit in relation to a range of social practices are themselves linked to larger structures of identity. What is usually cited here are structures like class, ethnicity, race, gender and sexuality. It is important to mention that these different forms of identities are not discrete – they interact with each other.

A further development of this concern with the interfusing of identities has emphasized the hybridity of cultural identities. The notion of hybridity suggests that identities are not pure but the product of mixing fusion. Underlying this account of identity is an attention to the mixing and movement of cultures. The most prominent among these diverse forms of cultural traffic is the contemporary circulation of various channels of mass media. The resulting fusion or hybridity of identities is not the product of the assimilation of one culture or cultural tradition by another, but the production of something new.

Therefore, identity in modern sociology is used widely and loosely with reference to one's sense of self, and one's feelings and ideas about oneself, as for example 'gender identity' or 'class identity'. It is sometimes assumed that our identity comes from the expectations attached to the social roles that we occupy; which we then internalize, so that it is formed through the process of socialization. Alternatively, it is assumed that we construct our identities more actively out of the materials presented to us during socialization, or in our various roles. Goffman's (1959) work looks at the complex ways in which we present ourselves to other people – a process that might be termed as 'identity management'.

Further, at any given moment, identity of a social geography by birth, that is, 'national identity' is only one competing subject position among many others. This is a stance underlined by Giddens (1990) where he argues that, for most people most of the time 'national identity' is not at the forefront of their minds. Identity and meaningful experience are much more likely to arise in the realms of the private spheres of family, friends and sexual relationships. Since day-to-day life is one that geared to routine, national sentiments are not only distinct from them but tend to rise and fall according to the circumstances.

In the final analysis we may conclude that identity is the subjective conception of the self and personhood; it has to do with who one thinks he/she is, what one believes and what one does, and the way in which one makes sense of his/her everyday existence. Identity dwells in the realm of the individual's personal notions on the composition of one's social subjectivity and image both in external appearance and in internal worth. Individuals can acquire multiple identities according to varying situations and status. Identity is defined on the basis of variables such as class position, gender, religion, caste, education, generational status, etc. The formation of identity is a dynamic process in the sense that it is evolving and being constructed according to the interactions and exposures to the changing conditions of the social circumstances. People are more likely to self-actualize to discover an inner self, which can not be artificially imposed by tradition, culture and religion. People also like to embark upon quests for individuality and self-understanding. Some are conscious of this subjective process while others are not. Identity, which includes psychosocial aspects, entails personal as well as collective dimensions with reference to a community/society and having a culture of its own.

In the contemporary social scenario, the problem of identity depends on how an individual constitutes, perceives, interprets and presents oneself to others and to the self. As noted, for modern theorists, identity is a discovery and affirmation of an innate essence, which determines what I am, while for others identity is a construct and a creation from available social roles and material. Contemporary postmodern thought has by and large rejected the modern essentialist and rationalist notion of identity and builds on the constructivist notion, which in turn problematizes the issue of identity. Hence, the major task ahead of us is to explicate how identity is formulated in postmodern notions and is constructed in contemporary cultural forms. The basic question is whether identity is fundamentally different in the so-called postmodernity and whether a distinction between modernity and postmodernity and a distinction between modern and postmodern identities can be sustained.

Identity and the Middle Class

Class was never a simple, unitary concept. It was always difficult to define. In social science literature and other writings, 'middle class' as somewhat elusive social section has appeared as an uncharted but somehow significant social category for cultural and political processes across the world (Mills, 1951; Vogel, 1963; Singh, 1985; Wessel, 2001). The writings on the middle class in India advanced strong opinions on what the social and cultural characteristic of this class should be, but still employed the notion of the middle class as a rather loose category (Nair, 1974; Bardhan, 1984; Singh, 1985; Bhatia, 1994; Varma, 1998; Wessel, 2001). At the core of this discourse was an understanding of the social and cultural instability that middle class life supposedly brought with it.

The term 'middle class' has generally been employed to refer to that section of the capitalist society, which lies between the capitalist and the working classes. It has come to mean the professional or service class. This class may be demarcated from the other two classes, capitalist at the top and the manual, unskilled and semi-skilled labour at the bottom; by negative features that characterize the group of individuals who form this class; their income which is relatively large compared to that of the members of the working class is not derived from the ownership of capital assets but obtained from physical or mental human labour (Bhatia, 1994).

This class has grown in size over the last 100 years to such a proportion that many have started to doubt the wisdom of calling it a single class and prefer to designate it in plural terms as 'middle classes' (Nair, 1974; Singh, 1985; Bhatia, 1994). That has made the task of defining the class in concrete terms all the more an exasperating affair for the sociologists.[2] This is so because the middle class has now come to represent so great a diversity in terms of income, status, vocations, skills and educational qualifications among groups and individual constituents that it becomes difficult to group them together and designate them as a single social class.[3] Hence, Cole's (1950) earlier proposition that the term 'middle class' which "tends to become a merely descriptive adjective, designating those in the middle, rather than a term defining a distinctive section of the population" (p. 290), gains renewed significance and so this class as a social group denotes a not too homogeneous section of population. According to Varma (1998), the creation of a native elite in India in its own image was the most spectacular and enduring achievement of British colonialism in India. The intention to do so was stated without the slightest ambivalence by Lord Macaulay as far back in 1835. In his *Minutes on Indian Education*, Macaulay said, "We must at present do our best to form a class who may become interpreters between us and the millions we govern; *a class of person, Indian in blood and colour, but English in taste, in opinions, in morals, and in intellect*" (p. 2).

The conventional theory attributes to the middle class qualities of balance, prudence and stability. This point of view was probably first articulated by Aristotle who said that "the best political community is formed by citizens of the middle class".[4] In a more recent view, Bhatia (1994) confers two key attributes distinguishing this class from other social classes: its possession of education or knowledge in the broader sense of the term and leadership qualities that help to put the class at the top in all walks of life.

Modernization Project

Reflexive modernization postulates a sharp decline in the power and legitimacy of authoritative norms; a corresponding rise in a new form of identity formation which is oriented around the lifelong 'project' of constituting and exploring identities; and an associated decline in the capacity of social institutions to dictate people's biographies (Beck, 2000; Giddens, 1990, 1991). While these changes represent a kind of 'freeing' of individuals from institutions and normative constraints (Giddens, 1991), they also make people much more susceptible to the risks of their life decisions, notably in the labour market. The reflexive modernization thesis also suggests an entirely unprecedented and explicit intrusion of previously 'private' goals and aspirations into the 'public' world as people pursue their life projects.

The overall implication of the reflexive modernization thesis is a convergence of identities and experience, not least in relation to paid work, careers and family life. It heralds the end of authoritative norms and gender roles embodied in career models such as that of the 'organization man' in which women support their husband's public career by sustaining the private 'haven' of the family. Our identities are influenced, among other things, by what we consume, what we wear, the commodities we buy, what we see and read, how we conceive our sexuality, what we think of society, and the changes we believe it is undergoing. Our identities are formed, partly by what we think of ourselves and partly by how we relate ourselves to everyday life. Advertising, fashion, popular culture and the mass media are also powerful institutions to be considered in this regard. The consumer culture of the market puts on display a wide range of identities from which one can select one's own. Sarup writes:

> Commercial advertisements often show the commodities, which they try to sell in their social context (that is, as a part of a particular life-style), so that the prospective customer can consciously purchase symbols of such self-identity, as he/she would wish to possess. The market also offers tools of identity making which can be used to produce results, which differ somewhat from each other and are in this way customized or personalized. Through the market, one can put together elements of the complete 'Identikit' of a self. These merchandised identities become complete with the label of social approval already stuck on in advance (Sarup, 1996, p. 125).

Stuart Hall (1992) suggests that greater and greater numbers of people, both men and women, with however little money, play the game of using things to signify who they are.

There is an interesting anecdote told by Judith Williamson that lucidly draws attention to how objects are actively used rather than passively consumed.

> When I rummage through my wardrobe in the morning I am not merely faced with a choice what to wear. I am faced with a choice of images: the difference between a smart suit and a pair of overalls, leather skirt and a cotton skirt, is not one of fabric and style, but one of identity. You know perfectly well that you will be seen differently for the whole day, depending on what you put on; you will appear as a particular kind of woman with one particular identity, which excludes others. The black leather skirt rather rules out girlish innocence, oily overalls tend to exclude sophistication, ditto-smart suit and radical feminism. Often I have wished I could put them all on together, or appear simultaneously in every possible outfit, just to say, 'How dare you think any one of these is me. But also, see, I can be all of them'.[5]

Someone who has a choice of what to wear and knows the symbolic consequence of the choices could only tell this anecdote. The question is, "Does image represent our identity?" What the passage expresses are the ideas that persons are more than what they wear, that there is the possibility of multiple identities within the same individual. Perhaps, we would have to explore the range of meanings that a single object can acquire through its recontextualization in a range of cultural settings. We would then have to focus on how people experiment, like bricoleurs, with common materials, to produce a range of new meanings.

Tourists and Vagabonds

The idea of consumption and the formation of identity are linked to tourism that points to another dimension of image construction. Tourism in the age of globalization has become a commodity to be advertised, marketed and sold much like every other commodity (Bauman, 1998). However, what is not emphasized enough is the degree to which tourism can become little more than a means to seal lots of other commodities. For instance, a trip to Disney World is a desirable goal in itself as far as the Disney Corporation is concerned; but more importantly, suggests Ritzer and Liska (1997), it is the gateway to the sale of lots of other Disney products. The process begins on entering the theme park, which can be viewed as a thinly disguised shopping mall set up to sell primarily a wide array of Disney products. It ends with the Disney village marketplace, which opens late for those who want to shop after they have visited the park. Indeed, it is increasingly difficult to differentiate between shopping malls like Mall of America and these parks such as Disney World: "the former is a mall with an amusement park, the latter an amusement park with a mall" (Ritzer and Liska, 1997, p. 153).

Bauman (1998) takes this idea to a different dimension. He argues that like all other known societies, the postmodern consumer society is a stratified one. But, it is possible to distinguish one kind of society from another by the dimensions along which it stratifies its members. The one dimension, along which those 'high up' and 'low down' are plotted in a society of consumers, is their degree of mobility – their freedom to choose where to be. Hence, "in a restless world, tourism is the only acceptable human form of restlessness" (Bauman, 1998, p. 94). Another difference that is peculiar to this era is that those 'high ups' are satisfied that they travel through life to their heart's content and pick and choose their destinations according to the joys they offer. Those 'low downs' happen, time and again, to be thrown out from the site they would rather stay in.[6] Its side effect is the transformation of many others into vagabonds. Vagabonds are travellers denied of the right to turn into tourists. They are allowed neither to continue to stay nor to search for a better place to be in.

Vagabonds are on the move because they have been pushed from behind. The tourists move because they find the world of consumer culture within their (global) reach irresistibly attractive. The vagabonds move because they find the world within their (local) reach unbearably inhospitable. The tourists travel because they want to; the vagabonds travel because they have to as they do not have any other bearable choice. Hence, Bauman (1998) claims that there are no tourists without the vagabonds; as though, both appear to be the sides of the same coin that basically rests on the realm of identity although at opposing planes, so much so that the vagabond is the alter ego of the tourist.[7] Bauman further claims that both the tourist and the vagabond have been made into consumers today. The vagabonds are not really able to afford the kind of sophisticated choices in which the consumers are expected to excel; their potential for consumption is as limited as their resources. This makes their position and status vulnerable and so their identity in society becomes precarious.

Postmodern Regime

The debates among social scientists about globalization and postmodernity are closely related. Many authors seem to link globalization with postmodernity and the highly diverse and mobile cultural forms comprising postmodernism (Jameson, 1984; Harvey, 1989; Baudrillard, 1981, 1983). Nevertheless, postmodernity remains a highly contentious subject and many question whether 'postmodernity' *per se* actually exists, that is, as a distinct period following on from 'modernity' (King, 1995; Giddens, 1991; Tomlinson, 1999; Therborn, 1995). Giddens (1991) describes the late modern world as the world of 'high modernity'.[8] But writers such as Laclau and Mouffe (1985) and Hebdige (1989, 1990) have no doubts and mention that postmodernity is the result of changes in the social, economic and political processes.

Modernity[9] was marked as a historical period that began in Western Europe with a series of profound socio-structural and intellectual transformation in the seventeenth century and achieved its maturity as a cultural project with the growth of Enlightenment; and later, with the development of industrial society. It was associated with order, certainty, harmony, humanity, pure art and absolute truth. The oft quoted saying was that existence is modern insofar as it is sustained by design, manipulation, management and engineering. Whereas 'modernism' is a comprehensive term for an international tendency in the arts of the West in the last years of the nineteenth century and subsequently affecting the character of most twentieth century art.

One of the notable changes that mark 'postmodernity' as the shift from a Fordist economy to a post-Fordist one, based on information technology, robotics, diversity, decentralization, differentiation and globalization. Interestingly, Lash and Urry (1994) envisions post-Fordist 'disorganized capital' characterizing globalization having replaced old Fordist 'organized capital.' The post-Fordist regime is said to be of flexible accumulation, compared to the organized and more rigid capital movement of the Fordist phase, which is based on Henry Ford's model of centralized mass-assembly production of standardized products. The post-Fordist regime, according to Harvey, rests on flexibility with respect to labour processes, labour markets, products and patterns of consumption. It is regarded as the emergence of entirely new sectors of production, new ways of providing financial services, new markets and, above all, greatly intensified rates of commercial, technological and, organizational innovation (1989, p. 147). Postmodernity is capitalism in its post-Fordist guise and creates new opportunities, arenas and areas in which to operate but still driven by profit.

Empowered by new technology that has transformed production and, in the process, changed the composition of the labour force, capitalism has moved from mass to flexible production based on lifestyle and niche marketing. In this way, it has replaced traditional 'high culture' with a new aesthetic, based on the 'image industries', in which 'desires' are created over 'needs' in order to bolster demand. The key to the dissemination of such consumerism is advertising and the media, particularly in television, which now operate on a global basis manifested in the instances of fashion, pop music and lifestyle. Meanwhile, on the cultural front, postmodernism is celebrated by many as the end of modernism and the cultural styles and movements emblematic until the first half of the twentieth century.

Writers like Hebdige are strongly of the view that postmodernism holds out the prospect of genuinely 'new times' and of a release of genuinely liberationist as well as democratic forces. Various groups, such as youth, ethnic, gay/lesbian, etc., have used fashion and music to forge new lifestyles and identities (Simon, 1996).

A number of commentators have linked the rise of postmodernism to consumer culture (Jameson, 1984; Featherstone, 1991, 1992; Baudrillard, 1983). Both the terms 'postmodernism' and 'consumer culture' give a central emphasis to culture that pointed to two forms of contemporary displacements. In the purview of contemporary globalization, consumer culture marks a shift from considering consumption as a mere reflex of production to conceiving consumption as central to social reproduction. It points not only to the increasing production and salience of cultural goods as commodities, but also to the way in which the majority of cultural activities and signifying practices become mediated through consumption.

Consumption progressively involves in the consumption of signs and images. Consumer culture, in this sense, points to the ways in which consumption ceases to be a simple appropriation of utilities, or use values, to become a consumption of signs and images in which the emphasis on the capacity to endlessly reshape the cultural/symbolic aspect of the commodity makes it more appropriate to speak of commodity signs. The culture of the consumer society is, therefore, held to be a vast floating complex of fragmentary signs and images, which produces an endless sign-play that destabilizes long-held symbolic meanings and cultural order.[10] This key feature of consumer culture is often regarded as the central feature of postmodernism, which up to some extent was taken up by artists, intellectuals and academics in various ways as a problem to be expressed and theorized. Hence, there is the fragmentation of time into a series of perpetual presence and the loss/end of a sense of history. The inability to order the fragmented culture is also held to lead an aestheticization of everyday life through the inability to chain signs and images together into a meaningful narrative (Featherstone, 1995, p. 112). Hence, to a rationalized and at the same time centralized, clamorous and spectacular 'production', corresponds to another production, called 'consumption'. The latter is devious, it is dispersed, but it insinuates itself everywhere silently and almost invisibly; because it does not manifest itself through its own products, but rather through its ways of using the products imposed by a dominant economic order.

In his book *The Condition of Postmodernity* (1989), D. Harvey posits some kind of necessary relation between the rise of postmodernist cultural forms and the emergence of more flexible modes of capital accumulation – a new round to time-space compression in the organization of capital. According to him, the relatively stable aesthetic of Fordist modernism has given way to all the ferment, instability and fleeting qualities of a postmodernist aesthetic that celebrates difference, ephemerality, fashion and the commodification of cultural forms. Harvey looks at postmodernism as part of a history of successive waves of time-space compression generated out of the pressures of capital accumulation with its perpetual quest to annihilate space through time and reduce turnover time.[11] In this way, Harvey (1989) alerts us to the product of diversity now riding on the back of the increased speed of commodity circulation: "Improved systems of communication and information flow, coupled with rationalization in the techniques of distribution – packaging inventory, control, containerization, market feed-back and so on – make it possible to circulate commodities through the market system with greater speed" (1989, p. 285). The postmodern emphasis on ephemerality, collage, fragmentation and dispersal in philosophical and social thought mimics the conditions of flexible accumulation and consumption. This kind of situation necessarily generates a search for personal as well as collective identity.

Following Marshall McLuhan, Baudrillard (1981, 1983) interprets modernity as a process of explosion of commodification, mechanization, technology and market relations, in contrast to postmodern society, which is the site of an implosion of all boundaries – distinctions between high and low culture, appearance and reality. He argues that we live in a 'hyper-reality' of simulations in which images, spectacles and the play of signs have replaced the logic of production and class conflict. Using McLuhan's cybernetic concept of implosion, he claims that in the contemporary world, the boundary between representation and reality implodes, and that, as a result, the experience and the ground of 'the real' disappear. In this new social order, it is signs and codes that constitute 'the real'. The individuals are so caught up in a world of commodity signs, media spectacles, representations and simulations that there is no longer any access to a sense of the 'real' which is itself presented as an effect of the code or system. In such a world, everything becomes undecidable. It becomes increasingly difficult to distinguish true from false, or good from bad; because in the society of simulations it is impossible to gain access to a 'real,' or to perceive what is determining or constituting various events and processes.

'Hyper-commodification' regarded as the hallmark of postmodernism which Baudrillard (1983) terms as 'simulacra,' seems to shrug off the old elitism of high culture and be eclectic, playful, ironic and innovative in film, fashion, literature and architecture. It appears as though, in a postmodern society, incompatible worlds can coexist in the same space.[12] Thompson (1992), commenting on the dynamism of contemporary cultural forms, discerns cross overs between producers of the cultural artifacts and the general public such as architecture, advertising, fashion, films, the staging of multi-media events, grand spectacles, political campaigns, as well as the ubiquitous television.

One of the most frequent charges levelled against the postmodern culture is that it is 'depthless,' has little more than glossy appearance and illusion of superficial filmic images (Jameson, 1983); it is an attachment to cleverly crafted surfaces and effects. It is often described in terms of *mélange,* collage and montage. Descriptions of this sort, it is claimed, are capable of capturing the novel crossovers in musical forms, imagery, clothing, food and lifestyles which is now evident worldwide (Pieterse, 1995; Perry, 1998). Pieterse refers to the emergence of a global *mélange* as "cultures and styles collide and merge, [...] cultural hybridization reflects the mixing of Asian, African, American and European cultures: hybridization is the making of global culture a global *mélange*" (1995, p. 58). Its property as an insatiable appetite for media spectacles and scandals globalized by television. Robertson (1992), therefore, describes contemporary cultural globalization as nothing less than a 'postmodern game,' in which people worldwide are increasingly implicated and new traditions are constantly being invented. Cvetkovich and Kellner echo this view when they write that we are living amidst the "funhouse of hyper-real media images and the play of floating signifiers in the postmodern carnival" (1997, p. 11).

Commodity Aesthetics

Consumption in a postmodern regime seems to be tied up with the construction of a variety of lifestyles in acquiring and consuming goods reflecting particular tastes and preferences. In this sense, the postmodern can be read as the democratization of culture, individual and new avenues of political possibilities. It may be argued that postmodernism, whatever form its own intellectualising might take, has been fundamentally anticipated in the metropolitan cultures of the last twenty years, "among the electronic signifiers of cinema, television and video, in recording studios and record players, in fashion and youth styles, in all those sounds, images and diverse histories that are daily mixed, recycled and 'scratched' together on that giant screen which is the contemporary city" (Barker, 1997).

It is argued that consumer identity is primarily formed by commodity aesthetics; their relationship to the world is primarily aesthetic. On the one hand, commodity aesthetics is referred to as beauty – an appearance which appeals to the senses; and on the other hand, it refers to a beauty developed in the service of the realization of exchange value, whereby commodities are designed to stimulate in the onlooker the desire to possess and the impulse to buy. For instance, Bauman perceives that postmodern consumers are basically sensation seekers and collectors of experiences; they perceive the world as a food for sensibility – a matrix of possible experiences and they map it according to the experiences occasioned (Bauman, 1998). The emphasis is on the idea of aestheticization of everyday life that denotes the rapid flow of signs and images, which saturates the fabric of everyday life in contemporary society. The emphasis is also on the analysis of the transformation of reality into images.

Wolfgang Haug, in his book *Critique of Commodity Aesthetics* (1986), deals explicitly with 'appearance, sexuality and advertising in capitalist society,' which makes a valuable contribution to the understanding of identity. Commodity aesthetics determines the direction that an individual follows. First of all, new commodities make the necessary chores much easier, and then the chores make it inevitable to buy the commodities. Finally, what is necessary cannot be distinguished from what is unnecessary. The ideal of commodity aesthetics is to deliver the absolute minimum of use value, disguised and staged by a maximum of seductive illusion. Haug notes the tendency of all objects of use to assume a sexual form to some extent – tendency towards a general sexualization of the human condition. The general sexualization of commodities also includes people. With the help of fashion, it is possible to advertise oneself, above all, as a sexual being.

The propaganda for fashionable innovation is effective only when it influences the sensual being by playing on its desires and fears. What is being forced on the public is a whole complex of sexual perception, appearance and experience. Marketing sets a new standard in people's relationship with their bodies. Men and women are now obliged to maintain a certain image, as an attribute of their masculinity and femininity, which apart from the effort involved in cultivating the appearance, requires the continuous acquisition of a growing number of commodities. The emphasis here is on youthfulness as a special category and phase in the domain of consumer culture. Youth becomes stereotype not only for commercial success, but also for sexual attraction; and thus, for what appears to be happiness and success. The new formula that the consumer culture demonstrates is that being young equals being sexually attractive. As a result, with the threat of sexual ageing and the consequent isolation, there spreads a universal compulsion for people to decorate both of themselves and the interior of their homes with 'cosmetics'.

This quest for appearance is closely linked to the notion of 'lifestyle'. Lifestyles are routinized practices, the routines incorporated into habits of dress, eating, modes of acting and favoured milieu or encountering others; but the routines followed are reflexively open to change in the light of the mobile nature of self-identity. It is not a term, which has much applicability to traditional cultures, because it implies choice within a plurality of possible options, and it is 'adopted' rather than 'handed down'. According to Giddens (1991), under conditions of high modernity, people in general follow lifestyles; sometimes in an important sense, they are forced to do so. We have no choice but to choose. So, a lifestyle can be defined as a more or less integrated set of practices which an individual embraces, not only because such practices fulfil utilitarian needs, but also because they give material form to a particular narrative of self-identity. Each of the small decisions a person makes every day – what to wear, what to eat, how to conduct himself at work, whom to meet with contributions to such routines. Giddens adds, "all such choices (as well as larger and more consequential ones) are decisions not only about *how to act but whom to be*. The more post-traditional the settings in which an individual moves, the more the lifestyle concern the very core of self-identity, its making and remaking" (Giddens, 1991, p. 81).

In this context, Haug (1986) deals with the issue of self-presentation. He describes in detail how the salesroom is designed as a stage – 'a stage for entertainment'. Clothes are advertised like packaging as a means of sales promotion. There is an emphasis on physical appearance, on how the skin feels and smells, the colour, sheen and cut of hair. By gaining a new face, one simultaneously loses one's own. The body shares a similar fate. Consumer culture homes in on fears and unsatisfied longings, redirecting action and defining the body in a new way – both its look and its smell, as well as its tactile sense and self-perception. These are some of the ways in which commodity aesthetics takes possession of people. Moreover, maintaining the packaging is not only expensive but also it keeps one occupied. Haug's thesis tries to undermine the barrier between 'outside' and 'inside', between social production and human psychology. He successfully shows how the development of modern commodity forms, dominated by exchange value, intersects directly with the realm of human needs and the domain of sensuality. Everything, he says, implies identity and identity formation. At this point, we need to elaborate the theoretical and conceptual framework that links the notions of consumer culture, consumption and identity.

Notes

1. Dreze and Sen attempted to cite a detailed discussion on the overall rate of economic growth since the move towards liberalization vis-à-vis India's growth record in social opportunities and poverty removal. See Dreze and Sen (2002), pp. 315–333.
2. Vogel (1963) speaks of the emergence of a 'new middle class' in the context of the social developments that occurred since the second half of the last century in Japan and South Korea, respectively.
3. The vast spectrum of today's middle class ranges from Pranab Bardhan's 'dominant proprietary classes' (namely, the industrial capitalists, the rich farmer and the professionals both civilian and military including white-collar workers to blue-collar workers in the organized industrial sector, managerial cadre employees of both private and public sector enterprises, opinion makers and middle peasants in the rural areas (see Bardhan, 1984, *The Political Economy of Development in India,* Delhi: OUP)
4. Quoted in Varma, 1998, p. 27.
5. Judith Williamson, *Consuming Passions,* London: Marion Boyars, 1986, p. 91.
6. For example, in 1975, there were two million forced emigrants – refugees under the care of the High Commission set up by the UN for that purpose. In 1995, there were 27 million of them. If they do not move, it is often the site that is pulled from under their feet, so it feels like their being on the move anyway (Bauman, 1998, pp. 86–87).
7. For a detailed discussion, see Bauman (1998), pp. 92–93.
8. According to Giddens, postmodernism is best understood as 'radicalized modernity,' that is modernity coming to terms with its own intrinsic reflexivity.
9. For an elaborate discussion, see *Modernity and Ambivalence* (1991) by Zygmunt Bauman and *The Condition of Postmodernity* (1989) by Harvey.

10. Baudrillard (1983)and Jameson (1984) develop this argument.
11. Harvey and Jameson are in broad agreement: they both see postmodernism as a cultural expression of the economic changes taking place within capitalism. ... Harvey being a geographer, emphasizes the effects of time-space compression, and sees postmodernism as a historical-geographical condition of a certain sort.
12. It is common practice now, for example, to use the emotive appeal of classical music to advertise and sell cars, or link an operatic area to a globally televised sporting.

CHAPTER 3

Imagined World

Globalization, as it is in currency today, emerged primarily out of two interconnected historical developments: first, the advancement of technologies in the fields of communication, information and transportation; and second, the implementation of liberalized policies and the opening up of local markets to international flows of goods, services, technologies, and especially capital (Held, 1995; McMichael, 1996; Vera-Toscano and Chapman, 1999). However, economic globalization constitutes the core of the current process of globalization. But global trade networks have always been a part of the modern world. The recent wave of economic globalization is fundamentally different from its earlier manifestations. It is the unprecedented intensification and acceleration of an ever more open flow of communication and movement of people, capital, technologies, goods, images, and knowledge beyond national borders. As a result, there operates a global marketplace as against the international trade networks of the past, which binds producers and consumers across the world through a chain of commodity exchanges. The global labour force is also dispersed along the production links of these commodity chains (McMichael, 1996).

The cultural purview of globalization has opened up the whole gamut of consumption as constituent of the normative behaviour that primarily signifies one as a member of society. In a globalized market culture, the consumer cannot avoid the obligation to consume. Consumption has emerged as the principal mode of social integration and hence the purview of key ethical arena of behaviour within a society. In other words, individuals, all over the globe today, are primarily socialized into consumer culture. While the excitement and brashness of consumer culture has an undoubted appeal, it erodes a public space based on the ideal of rationality. While consumers may be critical decoders of advertisements, multinationals who are not subjected to any kind of democratic control and whose prime concern is profit, shape the terrain.

The consumer culture dream worlds – the arcades and departmental stores – were the examples of materializations of the phantasmagoria, which Marx talked about as "the fetishism of commodities" in *Capital* (Vol. 1). The new departmental stores and arcades were temples in which goods were worshipped as fetishes. The mass media of the twentieth century along with the Hollywood films, the growing advertising industry and television, could replicate this commodity world endlessly.

The global media has the effect of blurring the division between the realistic and the fictional. An important facet of the world we live in today is that many persons on the globe live in the 'imagined worlds' of the official mind and of the entrepreneurial mentality surrounding them. Beck (2000) picks up the notion of 'possible lives' and suggests that personal identity is to be understood less in terms of geography, nation, ethnicity and culture, but more in terms of how people dream: "More people in more parts of the world dream of and consider a greater range of possible lives than they have ever done before. The spectacle through which people perceive and evaluate their lives, hopes, setbacks and the present situations are made up of the prisms of possible lives, which television constantly presents and celebrates."

Tele-Visual Reality

Evolution of *tele-vision* as a fundamental commercial form has placed advertising in the visible forefront of its activities. Television remains the central vehicle for international advertising in both of its multi-local and global branding forms; television's organizational forms and programming strategies are mainly structured by the advertising industry (Barker, 1997). Though global branding remains a limited phenomenon, television is central to the production and reproduction of a postmodern 'promo culture' centred on the use of visual imagery to create value-added brands and commodity signs.

Since the centrality of the commercial manipulation of images takes place through advertising, media and displays, therefore, performances and spectacles of the urbanized fabric of daily life entails a constant re-working of desires through images. Hence, the consumer society should not be regarded as only releasing a dominant materialism; it also confronts people with dream images which speak to desires, aestheticize and de-realize reality (Haug, 1986, 1987). This aspect has been taken up later by Baudrillard and Jameson, who emphasize the new and central role, which images play in the consumer society that gives culture an unprecedented importance. For Baudrillard, it is built-up, dense and seamless; the all-encompassing extent of the production of images that has pushed it towards a qualitatively new society wherein the distinctions between reality and image become effaced and in this way everyday life becomes aestheticized.

The theorization of this process has drawn much from Marx's theory of the fetishism of commodities which had been first developed in various ways by Lukacs, the Frankfurt School, and later by Lefebvre (1971), Appadurai (1991, 1996a), Haug (1987), Baudrillard (1981, 1983) and Jameson (1983, 1984). For Adorno (1984), the increasing dominance of exchange value not only obliterated the original use value of things and replaced it by abstract exchange value, but also it left the commodity free to take on an ersatz or secondary use value which Baudrillard, afterwards, referred as 'sign value'.

Based on the argument on Marx's view of the fetishism of the commodity, Appadurai (1996a) suggests that this fetishism has been replaced in the world at large with two mutually supportive descendants: production fetishism and the fetishism of the consumer. Production fetishism is an illusion created by contemporary trans-national production loci that masks trans-local capital, trans-national earning flows, global management and often far away workers (those are engaged in various kinds of high-tech putting-out operations) in the idiom and spectacle of local control, national productivity and territorial sovereignty. To that extent the various kinds of free-trade zones have become the models for production at large; especially for high-tech commodities, production itself has become a fetish obscuring not only social relations as such, but also the relations of production, which are increasingly become trans-national. The locality, both in the sense of the local factory or site of production and in the extended sense of the nation-state, becomes a fetish that disguises the globally dispersed forces which actually drive the production process. This generates alienation, in the Marxian sense, twice intensified, because its social sense is now compounded by a complicated spatial dynamic that has gradually becomes global.

As for the fetishism of the consumer, Appadurai (1996a) submits that the consumer has been transformed through commodity flows and the mediascapes, especially of advertising, that accompany them into a sign. He writes: "Global advertising is the key technology for the worldwide dissemination of a plethora of creative and culturally well-chosen ideas of consumer agency. These images of agency are increasingly distortions of a world of merchandising, so subtle that the consumer is consistently helped to believe that he or she is an actor, where, in fact, he or she is at best a chooser" (1990, p. 99).

Commodity Signs

A key figure in the debates exploring the cultural process which links globalization and identity construction is undoubtedly the French semiologist Jean Baudrillard. Baudrillard was arguably the most important and provocative media culture theorist. His studies of simulation, implosion, hyper-reality, and the effects of the new communication, information, and media technologies blazed new paths in contemporary social theory. His claim of a radical break and rupture with modern societies won him acclaim as the prophet of postmodernity in avant-garde theoretical circles throughout the world. He proclaimed the disappearance of the subject, political economy, meaning, truth and the social in contemporary social formations.

Baudrillard views that consumption is seen to play the critical role in defining people's identities and consciousness, so that styles of consumption are held to have superseded the old class consciousness. In his early work, Baudrillard was much influenced by Thorstein Veblen's *Theory of the Leisure Class* (1899). Whereas in Veblen's book display is confined to the upper classes, Baudrillard considers the entire society as organized around consumption and display of commodities, through which individuals gain identity and prestige. Baudrillard provides us a compelling theory of commodity culture in which the world is constructed out of 'simulacra' (or simulations), which have no foundation in any reality except their known images. In his view, mass media is not a means of communication since there is no dialogue or feedback. Rather, it is a carefully constructed entertainment.

In his earlier writings on the consumer society, Baudrillard developed a theory of the commodity sign, through which he pointed to the way in which the commodity had become a sign in the Saussurean sense, with its meaning arbitrarily determined by its position in a self-referential set of signifiers. Baudrillard has pushed this logic even further to draw attention to the overload of information provided by the media, which now confronts us with an endless flow of fascinating images and simulations, so that "TV is their world". In *Simulations,* Baudrillard (1983) states that in this hyper-reality the real and the imaginary are confused and aesthetic fascination is everywhere; so that "a kind of non-intentional parody hovers over everything, of technical simulating, of indefinable fame to which is attached an aesthetic pleasure" (p. 148).

The emergence of a new postmodern society organized around simulation, in which models, codes, communication, information and the media were the demiurges of a radical break with modern societies. In his postmodern funhouse, subjectivities are fragmented and lost, and a new experience about the self appeared. Kellner observed that "Baudrillard's postmodern universe is also one of hyper-reality, in which models and codes determined thought and behaviour, and in which media of entertainment, information and communication provided experience more intense and involving than the scenes of banal everyday life" (1995, p. 297). He argued that reality joining with a media-generated 'hyper-reality' has resulted in a 'decomposition of cultural meanings'. In this postmodern world, individuals abandoned the 'desert of the real' for the ecstasies of hyper-reality and a new realm of computer, media and technological experience.

Baudrillard's work is valuable in that particular field where he draws attention to the increasingly fundamental role of signs and images in the contemporary world. In his early works during the sixties and seventies, Baudrillard merged the Marxian critique of capitalism with studies on consumption, fashion, media, sexuality and the consumer society. These texts can be read as a reconstruction of Marxian theory in the light of the new social conditions appearing in France in particular and the world at large in general. He was influenced by the work of Henri Lefebvre and Roland Barthes.

Roland Barthes is well-known for his analyses of the way in which the mythologies of advertising, fashion, popular culture and the mass media tried to transform petty-bourgeois culture into a universal 'nature'. He saw these mythologies/ideologies as naturalizing contemporary bourgeois society, making it appear that a historically-produced society was an expression of nature by erasing and covering over contradictions, or making them appear 'normal'. At its best, Baudrillard's early work provides the sort of critical theory and concrete analysis of everyday life and the social world produced by Lefebvre and Barthes.

Influenced by the structural linguistics of Saussure, Baudrillard (1981) argues that commodities are structures made into a system of sign values governed by rules, codes and a social logic. What are sign values? Marx analysed the commodity in terms of 'use value' and 'exchange value'. Use value was defined by the use and enjoyment of a commodity in everyday life, whereas exchange value was defined by its worth in the marketplace. Based on the Marx's concept of use value and exchange value, Baudrillard prepared the concept 'sign value.' Sign values are socially constructed prestige values, which are appropriated and displayed in consumption. As classical political economy claims, commodities are not the locus of the satisfaction of needs, but they confer social meaning and prestige, which serve as indices of social standing in the consumer society.

This theory implies that certain objects or brands are chosen over others because of their sign value – that is, their relative prestige over other brands or types of commodities. Hierarchies of sign values constitute consumer societies in which one's social standing and prestige are determined by where one stands within the semiological system of consumption and sign values. Against classical Marxism, Baudrillard argues that the object of political economy should be conceptualized as a sign as well as a commodity; at the same time he suggests semiologists that objects may be regarded as commodities as well as signs. Baudrillard's analysis of consumption provides a useful supplement to classical Marxism: through objects, a stratified society speaks.

Using Jacques Lacan's concepts of 'the mirror stage' and 'the imaginary',[1] Baudrillard (1975) argues that, in Marxism, individuals come to an 'imaginary' understanding of production, labour and value where 'imaginary' is not the opposite of 'real,' the image certainly belongs to reality. This Marxian 'imaginary' speaks to what is wrong with life under capitalism, namely, alienated life. Yet, the Marxian 'imaginary' simply reproduces the primacy of production. Marx's productivist logic is reductive because it reduces everything to labour and the mode of production, and so cannot account for many social phenomena like communication.

In place of the domination of all human activity in capitalist society by exchange value or use value, that is, the idea that anything is valuable only when it is useful or has a monetary worth, Baudrillard proposes valorization of what has no value in capitalist terms except its symbolic value. He proposes a new term 'symbolic exchange' as sharply contrasted with production and consumption. The term derives from George Bataille's notion of a 'general economy', in which, expenditure, waste, sacrifice and destruction were claimed to be more fundamental than economies of production and utility. Both Bataille and Baudrillard presuppose here a contradiction between human nature and capitalism. They assume that humans 'by nature' gain pleasure from such things as expenditure, waste, festivities and sacrifices, in which they are sovereign, and are free to expend their energy excess and thus follow their 'real nature'.

Hence, Baudrillard contrasts his ideal of symbolic exchange with the logic of production, utility and instrumental rationality, which governs capitalist societies. He celebrates symbolic exchange. This includes activities like gratuity gift-giving[2], festivities, destruction, sacrifice and waste. In other words, it involves the giving of gifts or goods for no particular reason; the expenditure of time and energy for no particular purpose; and engagement in activities such as festive, destructive, or whatever from which one gains no benefit or profit and which have no discernible use. It is submitted, therefore, that the era of production is over and that now we have entered a new era in which the production of objects has been replaced by the production and proliferation of signs. That is, we live in an era in which the new technologies – media, computers, information processes, entertainment and knowledge industries – replace industrial production and political economy as the organizing principles of society. Labour, itself, is no longer a force of production but a sign among signs. Signs and codes have become the primary constituents of social life.

In such a society, images, in a sense, become commodities. This phenomenon has led Baudrillard to argue that Marx's analysis of commodity production is outdated because capitalism is now predominantly concerned with the production of signs, images and sign systems rather than with commodities themselves. The general implication is that through the experience of everything from goods to culinary habits, music, television, entertainment and cinema, it is now possible to experience the world's geography vicariously, as a *simulacrum*. The interweaving of simulacra in daily life brings together different worlds of commodities within the frame of same space and time. But it does so in such a way as to conceal almost perfectly any trace of origin, of the labour processes that produce them, or of the social relations implicated in their production.

Real vs Spectacle

Previously, the media were believed to mirror, reflect or refer to reality, whereas now they are coming to constitute a 'hyper-reality'. Baudrillard also observes the function of television and mass media as prevention of response, by isolating and privatising individuals or by trapping them in a universe of simulacra in which it is impossible to distinguish between the spectacle and the real. In such a situation, individuals come to prefer spectacle to reality. Through the media, we enter a new form of subjectivity, in which we become saturated with information, images and events. The media now provides a simulacrum of actual events that appears more real than 'the real', which they supposedly represent. We internalize the media and thus become merely terminals within media systems.

According to Baudrillard, in the new world of consumption, there are affluent individuals who are no longer surrounded by other human beings, as they were in the past, but by objects; just as the wolf-child becomes a wolf by living among them, so individuals become functional objects. He suggests that consumption constitutes a total homogenization and organization of everyday life. The consumer believes that possession and display of the signs of affluence will bring happiness and prestige. He argues that the entire system of production produces a system of needs that are rationalized, homogenized, systematized and hierarchized. Individuals are induced to buy not a single commodity but an entire system of objects and needs through which one differentiates oneself socially, yet integrates oneself into the consumer society.

The distinction between appearance and representation is that representation refers to an original, a 'real', whereas appearance does not. Now, in our culture of information and mass media, we are inundated with an overabundance of images and signs that no longer have referential value; but, instead, interact solely with other signs. This marks the advent of simulation. Unlike the previous vertical connection between sign and meaning, there is, instead, the horizontal relationship of sign to sign. Baudrillard writes, "All the great humanist criteria of value, all the values of a civilization of moral, aesthetic and practical judgment, vanish in our system of images and signs; everything becomes undecidable" (1988, p. 128).

The process of simulation, the evolution from representation to appearance, is the result of implosion. Rather than the explosion of capitalism and commodification in the modern era, postmodernism is marked by an implosion – a collapsing inward traditional boundaries and binary distinctions such as elite and popular culture, appearance and reality, and so on. Implosion, according to Baudrillard (1988), is caused not by a lack, but by an excess of information. Here, we arrive at the source of Baudrillard's definition of the obscene as explicit or fully visible – that which is excessively available and made too evident. It is important to distinguish between simulation and the 'illusion' portion of the reality-versus-illusion construct. In fact, simulation displaces the entire reality-versus-illusion question. Simulation is the map that precedes and displaces the territory it once was intended to describe. It is one of the order of an alternate reality – the hyper-reality.

Seductive Value

At this juncture, Baudrillard (1975, 1981) contrasts the logic of production, which governs Freudian-Marxian theories of sexual liberation, with his own theory of seduction. In his work, the term 'seduction' replaces symbolic exchange as the privileged oppositional term to the world of production. Seduction is that which is everywhere and always opposed to production. 'Plato seduction' has become a polemical target of the philosophers who have worried about misguided souls being seduced by appearances and missing out on the reality behind the seductive veil of perceptual illusion. In the philosophical tradition, seduction is traditionally taken as the realm of artifice and appearance versus nature and reality. He does not interpret seduction in the sense of enticing someone to have sexual intimacy, but as a ritual, or as a game, with its own rules, charms, snares and signs; as one that is fundamentally artificial unlike the 'natural' pursuit of sexual power.

Media has the capacity to seduce us with its simulations, which can be more authentic than the original; and can undermine any contrast to the real by absorbing the real within itself (Poster 1988). As a consequence, in a tele-visual culture of simulacra, it is becoming more and more difficult to distinguish the 'real' from the fake, the hyper-real, which is increasingly becoming even 'more real' than the original. It is no longer a matter of the false representation of reality, but actually the real is no longer remain 'real' anywhere. Baudrillard's (1983) study of Disneyland illustrates how hyper-reality actually operates. Disneyland is a play of illusions, which encapsulates America's values in comic strip form and, in the process, conceals the contradictions in American society (Perry, 1998). Disneyland simulates a false, idealized reality by packaging what is understood as being the essence of a nation. Similarly, a soap opera may be fiction, but it is 'real' in its impact on its viewers. Media images do not merely represent reality. They are reality because their meaning derives from their position within a system of signs and not from reference to the 'real world' outside that system. Baudrillard argues that a multiplicity of constantly shifting cultural codes is at work and that there is no longer a fixed metacode against which they can be judged and to which they all relate. What is important to note here is that the notion of hyper-reality is, however, not just applicable to culture. The use of new communicational technologies in international financial transactions has given rise to a hyper-space of 'fast capitalism' as the global flow of capital, energy, goods and people speeds up to accompany the proliferation of images, simulations and symbols.

In his later work, Baudrillard (1988) elaborates the triumph of objects over subjects within the proliferation of an object world, which is so completely out of control that it surpasses all attempts to understand, conceptualize and control over it. He describes the 'fatal strategies' whereby objects come to fascinate, challenge, seduce and ultimately overpower the subject. He spoke about the theme of the growing power of the world of objects over the subject. The fascination of the objects has accelerated rapidly, and the subject has found himself or herself more and more immersed, plugged in, networked, and seduced by the work of things. The defeat of the subject by the object renders dreams of liberation a mirage and an illusion. It seems that Baudrillard has forgotten that it is impossible to envisage a world of objects without human subjectivity. However, here, we need to deploy a dialectical view. The subject, in a way, is an effect of objects; but at the same time the object is, in some other ways, an effect of subjects. This dialectical relation between the subject and the object, the perennial epistemological concern of any sociological gaze, has to be reckoned with.

In the above theoretical deliberations we are close to the central problem of cultural processes in the contemporary society. Culture goes on everywhere in social life, organized as a flow of meanings, by way of meaningful forms, among people. In the market framework, cultural commodities are moved and presumably carry some meaning. However, in some cases, intellectual, aesthetic or emotional appeal is all there for a commodity, or for a very large part of it and this is what we would primarily have in mind as we speak of cultural commodities. In a market framework, meanings and meaningful forms are thus produced and disseminated by specialists in exchange of material compensation, setting up asymmetrical relationships between producers and consumers.

In the first chapter, we have talked about the idea of the unprecedented flow of culture in the form of commodities – both material and symbolic – across the globe, plucking it from a given locale. Thus, social anthropologists have come to conceptualize these motions of culture as the characteristics of contemporary globalization as 'reterritorialized'. The term refers to the process of reinscribing culture in new time-space contexts of relocalizing it in specific cultural environments. The point is that globalized culture is never simply deterritorialized. It is always reterritorialized. These two processes occur simultaneously. In a way, it is a double movement with the neologism of deterritorialization. The term captures at once the lifting of cultural subjects and objects from fixed spatial location and their relocalization in new cultural settings takes place. It refers to processes that simultaneously transcend territorial boundaries and have territorial significance. There is no dislodging of everyday meanings from their moorings in particular localities without their simultaneous reinsertion in fresh environments.

However, the deterritorialization of culture raises concerns for the organization of the flow of meaning in the world, or what might be called the cultural economy of globalization (Massey, 1994). The fact that culture is being dislodged from one locality and placed in another, itself says nothing about the sort of culture that is being disembedded or about its origins and destinations. At this juncture, the question arises whether this dissemination involves some forms of asymmetry points to the relevance of power geometry of globalization. The discourse of cultural imperialism offers one perspective to the globalization of culture. One of the central propositions of this discourse is that the deterritorialization of culture is not a benign matter.[3] For, there is indeed power geometry being operative in the processes of globalization. It is one in which the traffic in culture moves primarily in one direction, sometimes it is seen to move from the developed world – West/Centre, to the developing world East/Periphery – at other times. In either case, given the asymmetries that putatively structure the flow of meaning, the discourse of cultural imperialism suggests that the processes of globalization involve the domination of certain cultures over others. In other words, this discourse perceives the increased global movement of cultural goods primarily as a process of cultural imposition and dominance, that is, the imposition and dominance of western culture over the remainder of the globe. This pattern of domination leads to a cultural homogenization of the world and the consequent global cultural influences continuously batter the sensibilities of the people of the periphery. Subsequently, peripheral culture will gradually assimilate more and more of the imported meaning and forms; becoming indistinguishable from the centre step by step. The deterritorialization of culture is thus conceived as promoting a convergence of cultural styles in as much as western culture is being embraced in localities around the globe.

This discourse presents us with two specific, albeit interrelated, visions of global cultural uniformity. The first vision attributes the increasing synchronization of world culture to the ability of trans-national capital, most often seen as American-dominated and mass-mediated, to distribute cultural goods across the globe. This monopoly has become so strong that the American broadcasting system, which is essentially a commercial system dependent on advertising revenue, has functioned as an archetype for the formation of broadcasting systems all over the globe, particularly in the southern hemisphere (Inda and Rosaldo, 2002). One problem with the dissemination and adoption of this commercial system of mass media is that it has opened up developing countries to the large-scale importation of consumer-oriented foreign programmes. The outcome has become an electronic invasion that promises to eradicate local traditions everywhere. Local culture, in other words, is meeting with submersion from the mass-produced emissions of commercial broadcasting. These countries have become strapped and buckled with an American-dominated global system of communication and commodity production, which threatens to supplant traditional cultural values with the values of consumerism.

The second vision of global uniformity attributes synchronization of the world to the spread of western culture more generally.[4] This means that globalization entails more than just the simple spread of American/Western cultural goods and more than the development of a global taste for McDonald's, Levi's, Coca-Cola, and so on. It involves, as Tomlinson points out, "the installation worldwide of western version of basic social-cultural reality: the West's epistemological and ontological theories, its values, ethical systems, approaches to rationality, technical-scientific worldview, political, cultural and so on" (1999, p. 144). In other words, globalization entails the dissemination of all facets of the West's way of being: from musical forms, architecture, and modes of dress to eating habits, languages, especially English, philosophical ideas, cultural values and dispositions – those concerning, for example, freedom, democracy, gender and sexuality, human rights, religion, science and technology.

Cultural Dislocation

The discourse of cultural imperialism admits the experience of deterritorialization as the global dissemination of certain cultural practices, goods, styles, institutions and so forth – the result being the increasing cultural homogenization of the world. It suggests that western culture, whether in the form of consumer goods or otherwise, has been lifted from its territorial grounding to be replicated across the world, leaving a trail of uniformity behind it. It presents not an entirely implausible scenario. The signs of global uniformity, at least on some levels, are there.[5] An important assumption of the future cultural imperialism discourse is that TV programmes, which are made for a commercial television system, will unavoidably express consumerist values both in the programmes themselves and in the advertising field, which constitutes the financial basis of the system. These representations will in turn create wants and foster consumerist motivations in their recipients in such a way that these recipients become harnessed to a western-based system of commodity production and exchange (Thompson, 1995).

It is criticized that the notion of cultural imperialism regards developing world subjects as passive consumers of imported cultural goods. It has been argued that the discourse of cultural imperialism relies on what is called the hypodermic model of media effects (Morley and Robins, 1995, p. 126). This model presupposes that media texts have direct cultural effects on those who view them. This means that cultural effects are imputed from an examination of the cultural forms on themselves rather than from careful attention to the actual context of viewing. It is submitted that the consumers of developing world faced with an imported text, media or otherwise, will not simply or necessarily absorb its ideologies, values and lifestyle positions. Rather, they will bring their own cultural dispositions to bear on such a text, interpreting it according to their own cultural codes.[6] Inda and Rosaldo (2002) prefer the term 'customization' because according to them it is less ideologically loaded than other terms.[7] The classic example referred to the process of customization is Liebes and Katz's (1990) study on the reception of Dallas in Israel focusing on four different ethnic groups: Arabs, Russian Jews, Moroccan Jews and Kibbutz members. The basic finding of the study is that viewers from diverse cultural backgrounds attributed very different meanings to the same programme.

Bauman (1988) considers the link between the historically changing nature of time and space and the pattern and scale of social organization, particularly the effects of the present-day time-space compression on the structuration of planetary and territorial societies and communities. Bauman traces the impact of the separation between the two settings in which the 'top' and the 'bottom' of the new hierarchy are respectively located in the changing organization of space and the changing meaning of 'neighbourhoods' in the context of contemporary metropolis. Bauman writes:

> The term 'time-space compression' encapsulates the ongoing multi-faceted transformation of the parameters of the human condition. Globalization divides as much as it unites; between them, the two closely inter-connected processes sharply differentiate the existential conditions of whole populations and of various segments of each one of the populations. Mobility climbs to the rank of the uppermost among the coveted values – and the freedom to move, perpetually a scarce and unequally distributed commodity, fast becomes the main stratifying factor of our late-modern or postmodern times (1988, p. 2).

Eric Michaels (2002), in his study on the reception of Hollywood videotapes among Warlpiri Aborigines in the western Central Desert of Australia, recognizes a good deal of interpretive activity on the part of viewers to supply contents as well as contexts with which to make the media events meaningful. However, these arguments do not lead one to conclude that foreign texts have no cultural influence at all. They suggest that the process of interpretation, i.e., the influence that foreign programmes have on their audiences, is rather more complicated than the discourse of cultural imperialism, which its hypodermic model permits. The homogenization scenario makes sense when it can be established that the consumers of foreign cultural products are internalizing the values allegedly contained in them.

Cultural imperialism discourse has been criticized on the ground that its vision of the world has to do with the tendency to analyse globalization as a flow from the West to the rest (Inda and Rosaldo, 2002). As a matter of fact, there is a substantial asymmetry in the flow of meaning in the world – the centre mostly speaks, although the periphery principally listens (Hannerez, 1992, p. 219). At the same time, culture moves in the opposite direction too, such as from the rest of the world to the West.[8] This discussion of reverse cultural flows again points to the fact that the process of globalization is too complex to be thought of merely as a westernizing affair. In other words, globalization cannot be conceived solely as a one-way matter – western imperialism. Secondly, the process of globalization cannot be thought of merely as a homogenizing affair. For it is also, up to some extent, heterogenization. Hence, Inda and Rosaldo (2002) put forth the image of 'dislocation'[9]. The world can be thought of as a dislocated cultural space insofar as global cultural power has ceased to be concentrated in the West and has become somewhat diffused. It can be considered dislocated to the degree so that the traffic in culture or the flow of meaning originates not only in West, but also in places all over the globe, and so viewing "the world as a complexly interconnected cultural space, one full of crisscrossing flows and intersecting systems of meaning" (Inda and Rosaldo, 2002, p. 26).

In the final analysis, the term 'culture' refers to the way in which a human group lives, thinks, feels, organizes (itself), celebrates and shares life. Underlying all manifestations and expressions of culture, there is a system of meanings, of values and criteria, of world views that are translated into languages, gestures, symbols, roles, styles and patterns of life, as well as into the perception, analysis, interpretation and evaluation of reality in its action and expression. Hence, culture is taken to mean attitudes, values and mentalities, as they are expressed, embodied and symbolized in artefacts, performances and the practice of everyday life. Culture is a collective mode of life or a repertoire of beliefs, styles, values and symbols. We can only speak of cultures, never just culture; for a collective mode of life, or a repertoire of beliefs, etc., presupposes different modes and repertoires in a universe of modes and repertoires.

Both the material aspects (art, craft, and technology) and the non-material aspects (value, attitude, belief) of culture are essential elements of human life. They make up the framework in which communities function by giving common meaning, interpretative function and value normative function for their economic, social, political and religious activities. Moreover, they operate through institutions like family, church, market, government, voluntary association whose processes can either develop or break down with the passage of time. In times of social change, they involve a continual re-evaluation of accepted practices.

By 'global culture' we mean a unitary world culture, or a bounded culture connected to a world state, when we are a long way from such a scenario. Smith (1990) has pointed out that cultures tend to be particular, time-bound and expressive of identities, whose historical circumstances have formed over long periods. Such cultural feelings and values refer to three components of shared experience – a sense of generational continuity, shared memories of specific events and people, and a common sense of destiny on the part of the collectivity. As yet, Smith argues, there is a little progress in the way of shared world memories to underpin a global culture. On the other hand, we may be able to identify global cultural processes of both cultural integration and disintegration, which are independent of inter-state relations.

In any given society, it is culture that determines and conditions the subjective identity of individuals as well as communities and renders meanings to their relationships, interactions and organizations. On the one hand, identities are shaped and tend to become meaningful at the subjective level of human nature and consciousness in the ambience of a particular culture, on the other, by sharing the collective consciousness emanating out of that given culture, defined by the differences of territory, ecology, ethnicity, language and history of the people in societies.

The task is to examine the effects on the formation of middle class subjectivity on account of global economy entering into the local culture. Baudrillard (1975, 1981, 1983) and others have reiterated the fact that the plethora of consumer culture is the privileged stage where the contestations and negotiations of identities occur in the present-day society. Identities are moulded as consumers; it is something we could call consumer identity. In a globalized economy, the middle class in India has been placed in the spotlight for an entirely new reason – its ability to consume. At the centre of this question of identity are issues, such as who or what, influences and defines the identity of individuals and social groups in the globalized scenario of contemporary society. The following chapters, founded on empirical data base, are an attempt in this direction.

Notes

1. See Jacques Lacan, *Ecrits: A Selection,* London: Tavistock, 1977, pp. 1–7.
2. The gift, though formally gratuitous, is in effect obligatory; the gift is never free. See Marcel Mauss, *The Gift*, New York: Norton, 1967; the work of Levi-Strauss, particularly his studies of marriage exchange was influenced by Mauss.
3. See Tomlinson (1991) for a more nuanced view of this discourse.
4. This second vision of global cultural uniformity is drawn more or less from Latouche (1996).
5. Take clothes or food, for example: there are certain styles and brands that have become household names all over the world. Or take film and television: CNN, MTV and the Disney Channel are globally recognized icons.
6. See Ang (1985); Liebes and Katz (1990).
7. Other names for this process of interpreting foreign cultural forms according to local conditions of reception are indigenization (Appadurai, 1996a), transculturation (Lull, 200), and creolization (Hannerez, 1992).
8. For detailed discussion and illustration, see Jonathan Xavier Inda and Renato Rosaldo, 2002, pp. 18–26
9. The term 'dislocation' is borrowed form Ernest Laclau (1990), who uses it to refer to structures whose centre has been displaced – displaced in such a way as to be supplemented not by another centre but by a plurality of them. The main structures Laclau has in mind are modern societies or nation-states.

CHAPTER 4

Consuming Desires

When we stop to think, we realize that the 'electronic reach' of the Western products, like Hollywood, McDonald's, Coca-Cola, Nike, Adidas etc., is ensuring the spread of nothing less than a 'new world culture'. The consumer society, with its panorama of goods and services, transnational forms of architecture and design, and a wide range of products and social forms, is traversing national boundaries and becoming part of a new world culture (Cvetkovich and Kellner, 1997). For example, a global brand is available in most countries in the world. A global brand is one which shares the same strategic principles, positioning and marketing in every market throughout the world, although the marketing mix, such as price, promotion, appeal, media, distribution channels and tactics, can vary. It carries the same brand name or logo. Its values remain identical in all countries and it has a substantial market share in all countries and comparable brand loyalty. The distribution channels are also similar (Mooji, 1998). McDonald's depicts a good illustration of this unfathomable reach[1] and the use of global brands. There are marked differences in the added values imputed to global brands in the country of origin and management and in other satellite-consuming countries.[2]

People all over the world get exposed to the world of consumer culture through the world of media such as common periodicals, television with network of cable channels, Internet connectivity and mobile phone. The unprecedented explosion of information and communication technologies is truly shrinking the world resulting in a dramatic perpetration of global market into all realms of life in every nook and corner of the world. This is the manner in which cultural 'de-location' and/or 're-location' occur wherein local cultures can no longer be justified, shaped and renewed in seclusion from the rest of the world within the global context of exchange and dialogue. This aspect of penetration of the global market into the everyday realms of indigenous life, Beck (2000) refers to as *'globalism,'* denotes the fact that the 'world market' is powerful enough to supplant local and national political action.

Globalization in its contemporary wave thus involves a profound reorganization of time and space in social and cultural life. Perhaps as the earliest conceptualization on this changing notion of time and space, David Harvey (1989) explained it as 'time-space compression'.[3] He referred to the manner in which the speeding up of economic and social processes experientially shrinking the globe, so that distance and time no longer appear to be major constraints on the organization of human activities. It entails the speeding up of the pace of life, such that the time taken to do things, as well as the experiential distance between different locations in space, becomes progressively shorter. It involves the 'shrinking' of space and the 'shortening' of time wherein time annihilates space.

Mediation

In a global scenario, wherein unprecedented free flow of cultural artefacts occur, every nation and culture find pressed to stay open by the forces of media and technology that fuel consumer culture throughout the world and increase the cravings for new commodities and spectacles. The world of periodicals and magazines is a very prominent channel that disseminates as well as thrives upon the consumer culture and thus spreads the tentacles of globalization. This chapter attempts to make a closer examination of the role played out by popular periodicals in ushering and maintaining consumer culture within a given local context.

Coming from a well-to-do upper middle class setting, Maya is a regular customer of popular women's magazines. She revealed her interests thus:

> I read *Vanitha, Mahilaratnam,* etc., on a regular basis. Although we have got other periodicals like the *Week, India Today* etc., I may just skim through them. But I make it a point to read those popular women's magazines in Malayalam ... I have been reading *Vanitha* for a long time. I like them because they cover all the current issues of the modern age. If we look for so much of information and in-depth study in these magazines, we will not find those elements that an average woman looks for and are interested in.

Maya categorically pronounces that it is truly becoming an 'average woman' to be a regular consumer of popular women's magazines; and she identifies herself as an 'average woman,' because she is one such regular customer. Later we come to realize that the 'average woman' she refers to here, actually stands for the 'modern middle class women'. In the first instance, the latest brands and models of luxury commodities and services in a seductive wrap are advertised extensively through popular periodicals and magazines. It is quite revealing that 86.4 per cent (311 respondents) were regular subscribers to one or the other of the periodicals. In the case of those especially interested in reading popular women's magazines, the frequency revealed that more than half of the sample is regular customers. Nearly 59.7 per cent (215 persons) had made it a habit to read women's magazines with special interest, but 18.9 per cent of the respondents (68 persons) unambiguously declared that their prime interest in the periodicals was advertisements. It is indicative of the present-day trend of the middle class who was getting more and more attuned to the consumer world. According to Maya:

> They contain articles on family life, boy-girl relationship, sex life, pregnancy and child rearing, gynecological issues, etc. I take note of all these. Besides these, we have tips for cooking and the way special delicacies are to be prepared. Although I don't experiment with all that, I do make some attempts [...] then I like those special pages on fashions, models and

> advertisements. On the whole, the entire style and approach are very appealing. I also like other items such as tips they provide on how to be more beautiful and good-looking. I also try out some of them, especially for the pimples on my face. The problem with me is that I don't do it regularly and continue for some days.

Maya's reflexive comments tell us that in the context of the prevailing consumer culture, one has to read through the many and varied items found in popular magazines, especially in women's magazines together as closely related and mutually complementing. The sole objective of all those items could be seen as taking their root from one and the same motif, primarily devouring consumption. Thus, it is more likely that those advertisements, fashions and models that are normally found in the popular women's magazines are closely related to the latest notions on body, beauty, marriage and sex. Further, these notions are fed and cultivated by the world of movies with super heroes and heroines and mega stars of sports-spectacles. Hence, there appears a closely-knitted nexus among the commercial world of advertisements, fashions and models and the world of film and sports that is controlled and operated by market forces that disseminate consumer culture worldwide.

Occasionally, Maya used to tell me about the case of her niece, who just completed her graduation. She was more into the habit of experimenting with the tips and instructions on beauty and body care given in those periodicals and similar types of advertisements on channels. Maya told me once:

> [...] anyway I am not as crazy as my niece. She is very particular about those things that these magazines speak about. If she has to go out in the morning, she would get up around four o' clock and then do all kinds of things to beautify and dress her up. She requires a minimum three hours for her make-up. This is her routine. If she gets a pimple or something of that sort, she tends to be worried and insists on meeting a skin specialist at the earliest. Though her mother is a medical practitioner and child specialist, she is not happy with her; she has to meet a skin specialist by all means. [...] Now if you want to meet her it would be quite difficult; you have to get an appointment, as she would be normally busy with her

cosmetics and costumes. She is a first rate consumer of these women's magazines.

The case of this college girl illustrates that each of the factors in a popular magazine independently encourages the motif of conspicuous consumption, and they form an environment in which the propensity for vulgar consumption can flourish. So, these factors have to be taken care of together as a single and uniform cause that rationalizes the respondents' reason for getting exposed to the world of print media in general, especially the popular periodicals and magazines. In fact, 73.9 per cent readers (271 persons out of 360) appear to have a strong predilection of the contemporary popular magazines and periodicals on matters intimately related to the emerging phenomenon of consumer culture.

Image Industry

It appears that the growing national frenzy over sports (such as cricket and other spectacles in the South Asian scene), the growth in the domestic tourism, the penetration of the countryside by voracious media and advertising forces are to be viewed as an integral part of the one and the same process – the process of the engulfing extension of consumer culture, which has many other expressions as well. This is the process wherein images assume the character of commodities. In the context of the popular media spearheading aggressive consumer culture, Baudrillard argues that Marx's analysis of commodity production seems to be outdated as the post-capitalistic age is now predominantly concerned with the production of signs, images and sign systems rather than with commodities themselves. As against the logic of production, Baudrillard's theory of seduction (1975, 1981), based on Freudian-Marxian theories of sexual liberation, assumes greater significance in delineating these semiological aspects of consumer culture of the contemporary world.

This apparent tendency becomes clearer when we look at the main reasons for the high rating of certain magazines the respondents preferred (Figure 4.1). While 16.4 per cent (51 persons out of 311) choose to go through certain magazines

Figure 4.1

Preference for the choice of popular magazines

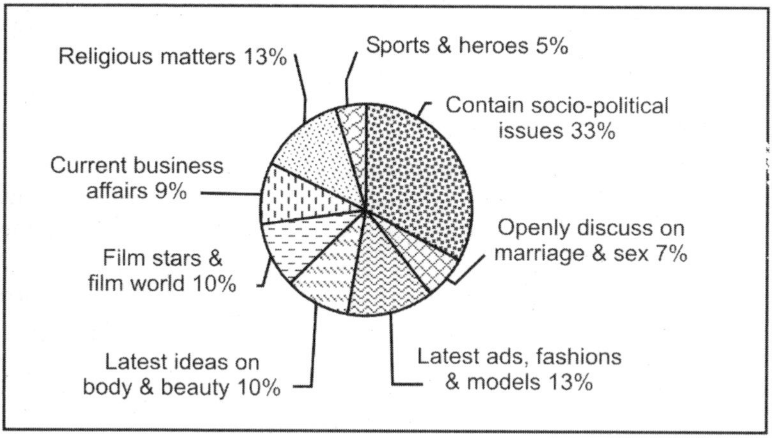

because they offered the latest ideas on body and beauty care, the same percentage of respondents preferred the magazines or periodicals as their best choice because they provided news about film stars and the film world, and still a slightly larger percentage of respondents, that is, 21.5 per cent (67 out of 311 persons), rated high those magazines which focused on sports and sports stars. To this number, 9.4 per cent may be added who were particularly interested in women's magazines just because they openly discussed various dimensions of marriage and sex. A cursory scouting of the features on the topics such as marriage and sex in these popular Malayalam periodicals will reveal the fact that they are mostly surveys and opinion polls conducted superficially and presented in sensational and sentimental wrappers that are capable of inviting momentary interest and attention. It is interesting to note that all the issues of these magazines would invariably contain one story or other on matters pertaining to marriage and sex. As part of the marketing and publicity gimmicks, these sensational items are normally highlighted with catchy captions and presented as title stories of the respective issues.

We have two representative cases to corroborate. First, Bobby, a postgraduate student in a prestigious college in Thiruvananthapuram. Bobby was elected as college chairman in the year I was conducting my field study. He was very much liked and appreciated by other students and proved himself as possessing certain convictions and opinions. He also cherished lots of dreams about life and used to share them with me. During a conversation, Bobby expressed his interest in reading popular women's magazines. He says:

> I like reading *Vanitha* and *Grahalakshmi*. I know many are interested in reading them. I usually look for experiences and anecdotes about marriage, sex and boy-girl relationship. [...] I like to see and watch ads too. Some are very creative and attractive, especially advertisements on soft drinks, soaps, bikes, new model cars, etc. We can watch lots of beautiful people ... *yaar*.

The second instance was that of Krishnan, a sixty-year-old man, working as a seasoned social worker and the training coordinator of a voluntary organization. The organization had a well-acclaimed training unit that undertakes training of the officers of the Welfare Department and other departmental staff in the government, community organizers and animators of various NGOs. Krishnan designs and coordinates those training programmes. Krishnan's wife is a trained nurse working in a leading hospital in Thiruvananthapuram. When asked him about popular women's magazines, he remarked:

> My wife reads women's magazines regularly. I skim -through them occasionally. I have good impressions about them. They give good ideas on family, problems affecting different age groups, sex, beauty, women etc. [...]. They have not influenced our value systems; not even my sons. But I know there are several cases where values are drastically affected and some are definitely influenced by the ideas and priorities that these magazines promote. But our choices are not affected at all. We do not buy any item just because it is advertised in these magazines with great appeal.

These deliberations reveal the fact that popular magazines capture appeal from people belonging to various age groups and categories of the middle class, including those involved in social work and training programmes. Krishnan had two sons and both of them were doing engineering. He bought a new bike for them recently:

> We got the bike recently because my sons aspired for it. The scooter that we had was old. They wanted to 'shine' (exhibiting vanity and pomp). For them it was a need. When their friends do the same it also becomes a need for them. We want to buy a car too. Now, we are not able to afford.

It is likely that the consumerist ingredients that the popular magazines prepare in an environment of consumer culture influence people in one way or other; even though they are not conscious of such an influence. An enquiry to find out the reasons for reading popular women's magazines showed that the majority of the sample preferred them because they discussed women's issues at large (Figure 4.2). Almost 67 per cent of the respondents in the quantitative data (215 persons out of 360) subscribed to this view. However, other reasons why some of them preferred to read popular women's magazines included the following points in their order of priority:

1. presented a modern image of women (42.8%)
2. contained latest advertisements, fashions and models (13%)
3. provided tips to be beautiful (11%)
4. friends, neighbours and colleagues of the same social class read them (4.7%)

Figure 4.2

Reasons for reading popular women's magazines

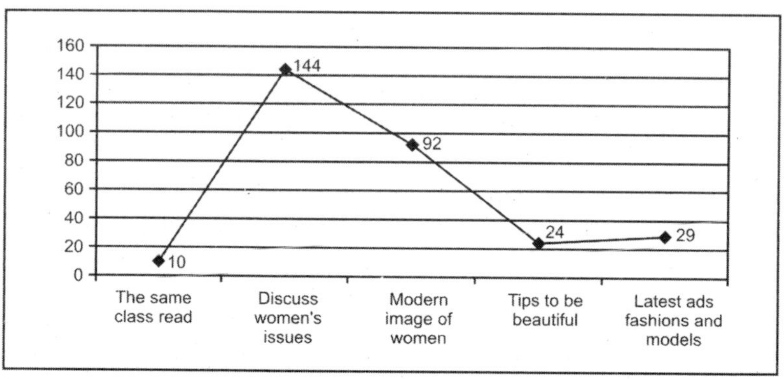

It is interesting to note that the highest percentage of the respondents opined that popular women's magazines present a 'modern image of women' (42.8%). The notion of 'modern image' requires further explication. Many in the middle class perceive widespread upward mobility combined with the advent of new styles of consumption as the defining characteristics of modernity. Being a part of the newly emerged consumer world and consuming its fruits is regarded as highly desirable, because it elevates one to be part of modernity and enhances status. Wessel (2001) in her study on the middle class in Baroda (now Vadodara) city said that a person who is able to consume successfully the new goods that have entered the Indian market gets stamped as modern and successful. "For this middle class, one qualifies as modern if one owns a car and goes out to eat in expensive restaurants, has one's house equipped with modern appliances and wears fashionable clothing" (p. 37).

Desire Kit

It becomes quite evident that there exists a close link between the commercial world of advertisements, fashions and models and the present-day notions of beauty, boy-girl relationship, marriage, modern lifestyle and so on in order to shape, condition and characterize the contemporary culture of consumption. Moreover, the force that controls and operates this worldwide dissemination of consumer culture is none other than the deep-seated commercial giants of the market. We need to see the organic unity in the content of the articles of these popular women's magazines and their other outer fittings like advertisements, tips on beauty, sex, marital life, love affairs and their preferred exhibitions of models, fashions, etc. In this sense, the entire percentage of the sample, that is, 59.7 per cent (215 persons) in a way fall under the same category who are wittingly or unwittingly well exposed to the global factors that disseminate and maintain consumer culture, which is an integral aspect of contemporary globalization and are accustomed to be the virtual clients of the same. However, the reasons that they acknowledge for this pronounced stance and behaviour appear varied and many, but ultimately all of them revolve around one and the same theme, mainly, become customers of a culture of conspicuous consumption.

Therefore, a close gaze would reveal that the ideas and opinions that these magazines convey through the features and articles that they publish and also other external paraphernalia, such as advertisements, models, fashions and other interrelated tips are centred basically on a single theme, specifically, the mantra of conspicuous consumption and the norms of identity and ideals of life and existence revolving around this culture of consumption.

Content analysis of a sample issue of one of the leading popular Malayalam women's magazines underlines this analytical perception. *Vanitha,* published by M.M. Publications, claims to be the highest subscribed women's magazine in the country. The issue under review is Number 25 of Volume 27, March 2003. The issue contains eighty-two pages including the cover pages and costs Rs 11. It comprises 16 features/articles including a novel and 20 full-page advertisements spreading over 23 pages and 13 half-page advertisements, thus making a total of 33 advertisements. The 16 items of 'matter' include wide range of things: 'the expectations of a woman from her husband', 'global impotency', 'pills for fertility control', 'answers to the questions and problems of teenagers/sex/pregnancy', 'tips for keeping the eyes beautiful', 'columns by and about cine artists', 'teenage fashion', 'story on traditional medicine practitioners', 'gardening and cooking', 'stitching fashionable dress', 'college girls' and 'world cup'. It also portrays the story of Kiran Bedi of IPS fame, addressed as 'the super cop' of India, visiting a women's college in Cochin. The inclusion of a sensational story of those girls who were adopted by foreign people, meeting their parents after many years who had abandoned them on account of poverty also attracts the attention of the reader.

A close look at those articles will reveal that the treatment in general is sensational and superfluous, so as to evoke a 'tickling' feeling in the consumer's mind. Moreover, the titles, captions and photos are framed in such a way that they induce naïve attraction and interest in getting hold of a copy of the issue. We find that almost 90 per cent of those items revolve around interrelated topics, such as man-woman relationship in the 'modern age' (16 pages), sex (7 pages), beauty (3 pages), fashion and teenager (8 pages with photographs of beautiful teenage girls) and consumption (14 pages). As usual, it also brings in the world of cinema (5 pages) and cricket (3 pages), which are inextricably interlinked to consumer culture.

A striking element of the issue is that it carries a four-page material with a number of colour photographs (11 demonstrations on specific modern and expensive gadgets and home appliances out of the 16 photographs in the feature altogether) of the 'Mega Consumer Gala' that *Vanitha* organized in Cochin. It was basically an exhibition-cum-sale of the most modern and advanced consumer durables and food items. Descriptions of the items and stalls of the foreigners occupied a prominent place in the feature. Some of the rare items are also included in the fair – fancy crystals, arts-cool air conditioner, travelling chair, bed air conditioner, mobile stove, magic heater, oxygen cylinder, etc. The middle class people would only dare to aspire these items, whereas those of the upper-middle class and above would think of possessing. In short, consumption, in the most conspicuous fashion, is depicted as something quite natural and praiseworthy affair today. Hence, the magazine seems to promote the message that consumption has emerged to be associated with the present so much that the consumers of the magazine are urged to see modern goods as necessities indispensable for living life that is appropriate for the contemporary world.

Coming to the details of the advertisements in the issue, one notices at the outset that they cover more than one-third of the total size of the issue. Most of the advertisements target on middle class women and precisely feature beautiful young girls and housewives. The advertised items are those that heighten the desire level of the targeted group. They include items such as cosmetics (7 nos.), jewellery (3 nos.), saris and lingerie (4 nos.), detergents (2 nos.), cookery and nutritional items (6 nos.) and home appliances (5 nos.). Ironically, the issue devotes seven pages to advertise the magazine itself. Of these, two instances are used for announcing the details of the prizes and benefits of the different gift schemes of the magazine. These enticing schemes are sponsored in association with different consumer agencies and enterprises. In short, the magazine as a whole may be said to be a 'montage' on consumer culture and each item of the page is linked to the item that goes before and after it, and everything together they form a unifying code of consumption at any cost.

From the above analysis, it can be ascertained that mainstream media stands ultimately for profit-making business. The world of media in a capitalistic economy is basically an industry – a commercial operation. It is also true that advertisements, particularly those belong to commercial nature, are very important for the existence of mass media in terms of income and profit and the profit is built on feeding on consumer culture. That is the reason, why in capitalist countries attempts are made by some agencies, motivated by social sensitivity and strict ideological inclinations, to bring out alternate channels of mass communication in both print and visual sectors. In Kerala, we find such fragile attempts, which unlike the mainstream media with popular appeal, do not thrive on commercial advertisements; they emphasize more on a thin audience interested in value-based and issue-centred analysis and viewpoints on social reality and its dynamics. And so, they will have only limited visibility.[4] However, these alternative and independent initiatives will have to be differentiated from those print and visual mass media channels owned and managed by the institutionalized party organs. The main agenda of such party media will be to disseminate, maintain and reproduce the respective party's ideology and interests. The alternative moves in the world of media come from a distinct lot that belongs to a genre of its own with less utilitarian motifs and commercial interests or political clouts of established parties with their parliamentary ambitions.

Buying Culture

I met Santhosh who has an M.Phil. in Business Management, working as faculty member on contract basis in the PG Department of Personnel Management in a prestigious college in Thiruvananthapuram. His parents are government officers. He has two younger brothers doing Bachelor's programme in Computer Science and Plus Two course respectively, and a sister studying in 7th standard. He told me that he took up this lecturer's post on contract basis, leaving a lucrative job as Industrial Sales Promotion Officer with LML Motors. He recalled, "Promote sales and enjoy was the slogan there; hefty marketing ... 100 kilometres speed ... celebrations ... drinks. ... Symbolizing the 'LML Freedom' that the company advertises with pride. ..." He used to undertake very aggressive promotion, going to big establishments like VSSC etc. (Vikram Sarabhai Space Centre, Thiruvananthapuram). But it occurred to him that though this work was monetarily very beneficial it was not ethically satisfying. Hence, he left that and took up this financially less attractive job. He seemed to be a person with a difference. He said:

> I don't have any interest in women's magazines. The contents are not good according to me. They induce behavioural and attitudinal change in us for the worse. The other day, I happened to see one copy of *Vanitha*. There was an article about love affair. That seems to prove that there is no real love now; only puppy love ... that is against our norms and values. In our tradition, religion has got a significant effect.

The earlier discussion on the nature and orientation of the popular women's magazines in the era of globalization revealed that they act as a carriers of the peculiar consumer culture characterizing the present-day society; and that they thrive on exploiting human instinctive propensity to get drowned in the flood of this culture by buying and spending conspicuously. Conversely, Santhosh represents a certain section of the society which appears to detest wittingly these women's magazines, which are found to be prominent carriers of consumer culture. Out of the total persons included in the sample, 40.3 per cent are found to resist the elements of that culture which these magazines serve as advocates par excellence, unlike the opposite camp, which makes a larger proportion (59.7%).

This aspect of resistance is evident from the reasons that are put forward for taking such a stance. Some of the most prominent reasons have to be taken special note of pertain to the realms of culture – objectification of women, superficiality and sensationalism. If we exclude the reasons 'can't afford' and 'not interested,' all the other reasons convey a message of purposeful avoidance of reading these magazines. It means that they do not read these magazines with a purpose. This purposefulness points to a sense of resistance to some factors noticed in these magazines, which are not appreciated. Thus, we recognize two contrasting responses to the trends of globalization which may be observed in the sample population report – a larger percentage of people showing signs of accommodation of the tendencies spearheaded by globalization, particularly manifest in the form of consumer culture, and a lesser percentage of respondents trying to resist them (Figure 4.3).

Figure 4.3

Reasons for not reading popular women's magazines

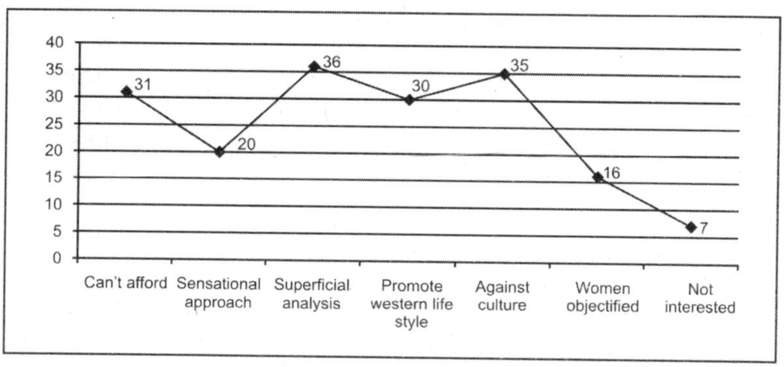

A comparative analysis in terms of education of the contrasting responses of the respondents by means of accommodation or resistance to popular women's magazines depicts a significant trend. In general, a progressive increase is noticed in the percentage of those who accommodate and resist, in proportion with the increase in their educational qualifications. From the tenth standard to the doctorate level, the percentage of those who resist is going down in comparison with the progressive increase in the percentage of those who accommodate (Table 4.1). The degree level is the most notable exception to the otherwise progressive and regressive pattern of tendencies of accommodation and resistance, respectively.

Table 4.1

Education-wise tabulation of those who read women's magazines

Read women's magazines or not	*Education*							
	10th	*Pre-Degree*	*Degree*	*Post-graduation*	*Technical*	*Professional*	*Ph.D.*	*Total*
Yes	19 51.4%	24 47.1%	77 64.2%	38 58.5%	18 54.5%	33 70.2%	6 85.7%	215 59.7%
No	18 48.6%	27 52.9%	43 35.8%	27 41.5%	15 45.5%	14 29.8%	1 14.3%	145 40.3%
Total	37 100.0%	51 100.0%	120 100.0%	65 100.0%	33 100.0%	47 100.0%	7 100.0%	360 100.0%

However, special note may be taken of the indications revealed at the professional level and doctorate level of education vis-à-vis the accommodative and resisting responses. It is at these two higher levels of education that the difference in the comparative proportion of the diverging responsive tendencies becomes most prominent. Thus, among the total 47 persons at the professional level, 70.2 per cent (33 respondents) belonged to the potentially accommodative category, whereas the remaining 29.8 per cent (14 respondents) belonged to the resisting category. In the same manner, out of the total seven persons at the doctorate level, 85.7 per cent (6 persons) belonged to the first category, and the remaining one respondent opted out of that group.

The gap between the proportions of those who formed these diverging responses seems to be prominently wide. In a way this is indicative of the fact that it is not possible to attribute a relation between educational qualification and the nature of response to globalization in terms of accommodation and resistance. However, a cross table analysis of this in terms of education and financial benefit revealed that there is no positive correlation between these two variables; therefore, education and income do not influence each other in respect of consumer behaviour conditioned by consumer culture.

However, an analysis of the same data in terms of the variable sex reveals a clear pattern of exposure to the changed market culture (Table 4.2).

Table 4.2

Sex-wise tabulation of those who read women's magazines

Read women's magazines or not	*Sex*		*Total*
	Male	*Female*	
Yes	102 45.7%	113 82.5%	215 59.7%
No	121 54.3%	24 17.5%	145 40.3%
Total	223 100.0%	137 100.0%	360 100.0%

Out of 137 female respondents (38.1% of the sample), 113 (82.5%) seem to be inclined in accommodating the pervading tendencies of consumer culture, whereas the remaining 17.5 per cent seem to take a position countering this trend. In the case of male respondents, the pattern seems to be slightly in the opposite direction. Among the total of 223 male respondents (61.9%), 121 respondents (54.3%) are not inclined to read those popular women's magazines, whereas 102 respondents (45.7% of the total male participants) prefer to read them. Hence, it appears that in the case of males, more respondents seem to be showing signs of resistance to the emerging trends of the new market culture.

Table 4.3

Income-wise tabulation of those who prefer to read women's magazines

Read women's magazines or not	*Income class*			
	Lower-middle (5,000–10,000)	*Middle-middle (10,000–15,000)*	*Upper-middle (15,000–20,000)*	*Total*
Yes	115 59.3%	68 58.1%	32 65.3%	215 59.7%
No	79 40.7%	49 41.9%	17 34.7%	145 40.3%
Total	194 100.0%	117 100.0%	49 100.0%	360 100.0%

However, at the income level, the emerging trend seems to be that the variations in the income of the different groups of the middle class do not likely to be particularly affecting the respondents' choice of reading or not reading the popular women's magazines. As Table 4.3 shows, the proportion of those who prefer to read women's magazine and thus accommodating the current trends of consumer culture is clearly higher in all the income groups, compared to those not inclined to read them. This indicates that income as a variable perhaps does not have any impact on the orientations of the middle class people towards consumer behaviour.

Table 4.4

Age-wise tabulation of those who read women's magazines

Read women's magazines or not	*Age Group*			*Total*
	15–30	31–55	56–70	
Yes	111 60.0%	92 59.4%	12 60.0%	215 59.7%
No	74 40.0%	63 40.6%	8 40.0%	145 40.3%
Total	185 100.0%	155 100.0%	20 100.0%	360 100.0%

The analysis of the data in terms of age reveals two things. First, in all age groups, a higher percentage of the respondents prefers to become a part of the current globalization trends by choosing to be regular customers of the popular women's magazines in comparison with those who resist them (Table 4.4). Secondly, it is interesting that the difference in the proportion of those reading and not reading women's magazines in each of these age groups is more or less equal, i.e., about 10 per cent. These two findings perhaps point to the fact that (1) age should not be considered as a major factor in the nature of response to the current globalization tendencies which would mean that the respondents' accommodative and resisting attitudes and behaviour are formed irrespective of their age; and (2) no significant difference may be noticed in the proportion of those who accommodate or resist the tendencies of globalization in terms of youth (age group of 15–30), adulthood or middle age (31–55) and old age (56–70).

However, an interesting trend can be observed from the analysis of the data on the percentage of respondents who resist reading popular women's magazines, in terms of sex. The sex-wise tabulation reveals that the percentage of female respondents is comparatively lesser in terms of all the pronounced reasons for not reading women's magazines (Table 4.5). The percentage of male respondents is higher, in respect of all the reasons stated earlier.

Table 4.5

Sex-wise analysis of the reasons for not reading women's magazines

Sex	*Sensational in style*	*Superficial Analysis*	*Western Lifestyle*	*Against Culture*	*Women as Objects*
Male	18 15.9%	30 26.5%	23 20.4%	28 24.8%	14 12.3%
Female	2 8.1%	6 25%	7 29.1%	7 29.1%	2 8.1%
Total	20 14.6%	36 26.2%	30 21.9%	35 25.5%	16 11.7%

Out of the seven stated arguments for not reading popular women's magazines, five of them are in one way or the other closely related to the impact of consumer culture ushered in because of globalization. The other two reasons, specifically 'can't afford' and 'not interested' may be excluded from this list as they are not directly related to the current market trends. Out of the five related reasons for not reading women's magazines, three are said to be more closely and directly indicative of the adverse effects of globalization, as reflected in the consumer culture. The objections are expressed in the following phrases regarding popular Women's magazines as they tend to (1) 'promote western lifestyle and beauty,' (2) 'disjoint from our culture', and (3) 'depict women as objects and commodities.' Although the net proportion of the respondents articulating these reasons is not very significant, it is noteworthy to find that in all these arguments the percentage of male respondents is perceptibly higher compared to that of female respondents. What is most prominent to note here is that the lowest percentage of female respondents supported the argument that "women are depicted as objects and commodities in the women's magazines", which is most closely and directly related to the existential predicament and identity of any women. Hence, out of the small proportion of 16 respondents who stated these reasons, only two were females, whereas the male respondents formed an absolute majority of 87.5 per cent (14 respondents). It is interesting to study whether this trend is indicative of the nature of identity construction of women in Kerala in the modern age of globalization.

Spybey (1996) suggests that the influence of globalization operates not only on the large scale, but also penetrates "the significant, the routine and the most intimate aspects of life" (p. 5). Beck (2000) points out that globalization "... can be grasped in the small and concrete, in the spatially particular, in one's own life, in cultural symbols that all bear the signature of the global" (p. 49). The dynamics of this dialectical process seems that the local as a micro manifestation of the global in that local everywhere can no longer escape the influence of global mass culture (Robertson 1992, p. 37). Underlying this issue of 'global-local relation' is the question of homogeneity versus heterogeneity. The idea of cultural homogenization submits that accelerating globalization in the form of global media, information systems and huge multinational organizations tends to erode local cultures and traditions. Beck (2000) captures this situation rather picturesquely: "In the villages of Lower Bavaria, just as in Calcutta, Singapore or the 'favelas' of Rio de Janeiro, people watch Dallas on TV, wear blue jeans and smoke Marlboro as a sign of free, untouched nature" (p. 42). Later, he refers to the 'single commodity world' where local identities are replaced with "symbols from the publicity and image departments of multinational corporations [...] satellites make it possible to overcome all national and class boundaries and to plant the carefully devised glitter of white America in the heart of people all around the world" (p. 43). More pertinently, as new geo-political and geo-cultural maps have emerged, the distinction between 'the local' and 'the global' has become less and less meaningful.

In contrast, Held et al. (1999) suggest that although national and local cultural identities cannot escape being influenced by global cultural flows, it does not follow that they necessarily reconstitute them. They argue that simple notions of homogenization, ideological hegemony or imperialism fail to register properly the nature of these encounters and the interplay, interaction and cultural creativity they produce (p. 374). Friedman (1997), in his study of a small Hawaiian village, mentioned that although Miloli is intricately involved in the larger world, its inhabitants protect and 'localize' their culture. These points to the possibility of cultural hybridization, instead of national cultures are destroyed. Cultural hybridization may be defined as a process of recontextualization and meaning re-attribution that signifies that foreign cultural imports are assigned fresh meanings within the receiving culture. The focus is upon reception and on the consumer's meaning-making, as they are inserted into new cultural surroundings.

Notwithstanding, in the process of accelerating 'coming together', which widely associated with globalization, there is a simultaneous 'fragmentation'. While nations are expecting to co-operate with states and regions, many of these are opting to advance their own concepts of nationhood. Nations are composed of groups whose common identity is based on a generally shared belief in a core notion of nationhood and these constructions of nationhood appear to be steadily increasing and regularly crossing state boundaries. In the 'new global order', nations and states are often in conflict and moreover 'nations' appear to be threatened with disintegration.[5] Instead of fostering unity, globalization appears to bring about increasing diversity simultaneously operating at various levels. Globalization is the reason for the revival of local cultural identities in different parts of the world. Local nationalisms spring up as a response to globalizing tendencies, as the hold of older nation-states weakens.

Notes

1. In 1995, McDonald's offered their services via more than 18,000 distribution points in 89 countries. In January 1996, McDonald's made it known that they intended to open another 2,500 to 3,200 outlets annually from 1996 onward. Two-thirds of those will be outside the United States. The company has standard specifications for its technology, product, client service, hygiene, and operational systems, but its communications are localized (Mooji, 1998, p. 142). For another illustration, take the case of Marlboro, which is treated as a premium brand everywhere. It is positioned around the world as an urban brand appealing to the universal desire for freedom and physical space, something that urban dwellers typically lack and that are symbolized by the 'Marlboro man' and 'Marlboro country' (Mooji, 1998, p. 141).
2. For example, Coca-Cola will have different meanings and values for US and non-US consumers. In the US, Coke is a part of the social fabric of Americana, much like McDonald's. Outside the US, Coke exemplifies the idea of 'American-ness' in its own way. Non-American consumers drinking Coca-Cola outside the US are quenching their thirst, too; but they are drinking in a little bit of American as well. In non-Western societies, especially, the brand helps in making inspirational American lifestyles a little more approachable (Mooji, 1998, p. 142).
3. For instance, Harvey (1989) illustrates: it is now possible for a large multinational corporation like *Texas Instruments* to operate plants with simultaneous decision-making with respect to financial market, input costs, quality control, and labour process conditions in more than fifty different locations across the globe.
4. Some such alternative outfits of the print media in Kerala are: (1) *Patabhedam* (Counter Lessons), Naithikavedi Publications, Thrissur (2) *ORA Massika* (Organ for Radical Action), Published by Forum for Renewal and Community Solidarity (FRCS), Paravoor, Alappuzha (3) *Keraleeyam* (Pertaining to Kerala) Published by Patabhedam Printers, Thrissur; (4) *Jananeethi* (People's Justice), published by Niyama Samskara Kendram Thrissur.
5. Examples would be the tension between Spain and the Basque separatists; Canada and the Quebecois; Palestine and Israel; Sri Lanka and the Tamil Tiger separatists; and India and Pakistan for Kashmir.

CHAPTER 5

Sponsored Subjectivities

What really distinguishes contemporary globalization from anything that has gone before is mainly the global impact of communications and transport, which has increased the speed and volume of the circulation of images, symbols, goods and people. No state is disconnected from global telecommunication and "even though most people remain rooted in a local or national culture and a local place, it is becoming increasingly impossible for them to live in that place disconnected culturally from the world in which it is situated" (Waters, 1995, p. 369). Both of the satellite television and its advertisements do have significant roles to play in the everyday existence, choices and behaviour of the middle class in the age of globalization. Annie shares the sentiments of a typical middle class woman and mother when she told me that she has no time to spend before the television. At the same time, it is a bone of contention for her at home:

> My children say that our TV is old model and pester me every time for a new one. They get the ads of various brands and models of different television sets along with their prices and try to impress upon me. [...] They are fond of dance, music and fashion of the latest kind shown in the TV. Then they want to imitate the dress codes and styles of the TV artists, if not outside, at least when they are at home. They also make

> demands for items that are seen in the TV; they ask for them repeatedly. After watching some ads on two-wheeler my son throws questions like "When are you getting a bike for me as a gift?"...

Commercial television has been considered as an entertainment medium par excellence. Television audience appears to be most entertained by stories, by narratives with familiar and recognizable characters, plot lines, conventions, and messages, as well as by familiar genres. Kellner (1995) has pointed out, "there is a new look and feel: the signifier has been liberated and image takes precedence over narratives, as compelling and highly artificial aesthetic images detach themselves from the television diegesis and become the centre of fascination, of a seductive pleasure, of an intense but fragmentary and transitory aesthetic experience" (p. 235). This chapter explores the role of this global medium of mass communication in the creation, diffusion and promotion of consumer culture of the middle class that go in the making of their identity. Hopefully, this enquiry will throw more light on the way in which trans-national satellite television participate in the remapping of cultural space in the era of globalization.

Fancy Park

Franklin is working as a Research Assistant in a Social Science Project. He is thirty-three years old and not married. After his Masters in Sociology he worked as a Research Assistant in about half-a-dozen research projects. According to him, in India, it is very difficult to get a decent job. There is no job security. He thinks beyond doubt that this situation is created because of the project of globalization and liberalization.

> It is high time that I got settled. I am now desperately trying to go outside India – Ireland or UK I have already spent so much of money for that but did not click yet. Now my attempts are to go to Canada; in view of that I paid Rs 75,000 in the embassy. I am trying to get an emigrant visa. When we go out we get better salary. So, we can spend some years there; afterwards, we can come back and live here nicely.

Franklin's elder brother went abroad recently and his only sister is also settled in England with her husband. At present, only Franklin and his mother are at home. Nevertheless, he changed his television set. He explained the reason:

> The old one was a Teltronic set and the picture was not very clear. It had only ten channels. Now, we got a new TV set that has hundred channels. It is like cartoons that we can watch war now. Without cable TV our knowledge of the world remains very poor. I watch sports channel too. As we watch, we become more interested in it. But my mother likes ads and operas. If electricity fails when operas being telecast, she is sad and telephones other houses and asks for the progress of the story. Without TV, life has become impossible. But, anyway, it is a costly affair which comes to about Rs 250 per month. Considering the cost factor, once we thought of even disconnecting the cable. But we could not stop it. Cable channels have become inevitable; yes ... in a way we are addicted.

These narratives inform us that television programmes attract every category of people – young and old, educated and uneducated, professional and ordinary. Ang (1990, 1996) has argued rightly that audience of mass media does not exist a priori. They are actively constructed through careful programming decisions and marketing strategies, as well as trans-national flows of information, capital and commodities. A narrative of the history of *Doordarshan* in India reveals some of the ways in which the 'viewing family' was constituted as 'national audience' through state policy, international communication organizations and trans-national discourses of modernity.[1] Bobby, who belongs to a middle middle class background, explains the manner in which cable television affects people in general as a universal experience:

> Almost every home has cable TV now. The programmes in the TV bring the feeling that those items are part and parcel of our lives which bring us prestige. Newer items are bought at home with a feeling that they are essential for us to enhance our prestige. I often feel bad when I am not able to adapt the lifestyle that TV exhibits as universal and common. The

> Veejays speak – *manglish* – stylized and pompous way of the use of Malayalam with a mix of English. In our lifestyle, as well as for our dress codes, we have a tendency to model TV-world as they are ideal and superior. [...]

Among various mass media, television now has the largest reach. Harvey (1989) observed that mass television ownership, coupled with satellite communication, makes it possible to experience a rush of images from different spaces into a series of images on a television screen. The whole world can watch the Olympic Games, the World Cup, the fall of a dictator, a political summit and a deadly tragedy. ... Mass tourism and films made in spectacular location, make a wide range of simulated or vicarious experiences of what the world contain available to many people (p. 293). It is observed that this is due to the shift in emphasis of government support from the other mass communications media to television. As a result, there has been a fast rate of expansion in the setting up of TV broadcasting stations, relay transmitters and earth stations in the last decades (Bandhu, 2001, p. 67). The Satellite Instructional Television Experiment (SITE) was a major landmark in the history of Indian television. Mankekar (1999) rightly observes that in its portrayal of 'modern' middle class lifestyles and its encouragement of consumerist desires, television seems to have played a crucial role in the cultural constitution of the middle class as a powerful historic bloc (p. 9).

The consumerist supports for such an outlook seemed to be well in place. Almost every consumer durable items could now be purchased on instalments. Enterprising firms started offering exclusive services for helping with the right loan for the right product from the right source. Consumer giants spent crores on advertising; the top ten of these spent close to a whopping Rs 600 crore in 1995 to target more consumers.[2] Substantially added to this, was the 'explosion' of satellite television. The 'revolution' commenced in 1991, and it was estimated that more than 18 million homes were wired to cable or satellite by 1995. Suddenly, a large number of middle class people, long resigned to the monopoly of Doordarshan, had more than fifty channels essentially supported by advertising. Some people in the advertising business have "lamented the prostration of Indian advertising at the altar of Western ad idiom and grammar."[3] The important point to take note of it is that the similarities are not merely in the superficial symbolism of advertising, but in the basic language and value system.

The impact of such depictions, in terms of the search for the desired lifestyle, cannot be overestimated. The Fifth National Readership Survey revealed that three-fifths of all urban homes had a TV set and that the reach of the medium had shot up from 9 per cent in 1990 to 74 per cent in 1995. Hence, burgeoning aspirations wrapped themselves with commendable facility around the most expensive goodies. Children absorbed the general mood of consumerist buoyancy far more easily. "The vision of the good life being drilled into viewers' minds is better internalized by children than the older generation," was the conclusion by the researchers (Namita Unnikrishnan, quoted in *Outlook*, August 28, 1996). It was also established that youngsters from middle class watched the most. Among this new generation of TV children, 75 per cent said that they wanted to own the products advertised on television (Namita Unnikrishnan, in *The Hindustan Times*, April 27, 1996).

One day, Annie was found a bit perturbed. Later, during a conversation, she told me that her children picked up a quarrel on the issue of watching TV. She continued:

> The other day my eldest boy was asking for Refresher to be kept in bathrooms, as TV educated him on the use of it and status attached to it. Soap, powder, scents, deodorants, etc. ... Each of my kids has their separate brands. They say that only those brands will keep them not only young, but also beautiful. So they should get that. Each of them uses separate brands. So much so that children cannot think of a life without TV. If the TV gets some problem, immediately it has to be repaired. My job is to keep children away from TV. Finally we cut the cable connection, because they watch all the time and don't study.

The quantitative data further informs us that TV with satellite channels is deemed to be a necessity for not only children of the middle class households like that of Annie, but also for all sections and categories of middle class in general. The response to the questions on the need and rationale for satellite channels unambiguously revealed the fact that an overwhelming majority of the respondents who constituted 85.3 per cent of the total sample, do consider that satellite channels are essential for their everyday life. The point that is brought out clearly here is that the respondents are quite sure of the importance of satellite channels in today's modern world. There is thus wide gap in the proportion of respondents who share the views that satellite channel has become an essential commodity in this age that is characterized by high level of consumption. Soaring majority opined that satellite channels are essential. They have enlisted the specific reasons why satellite channels are essential component of today's life. They include the following points in the order of priority:

1. information on worldwide events,
2. very informative,
3. highly entertaining,
4. without it poor self-image, and
5. advertisements on latest fashions, models and new products across the world.

It is very clear that the middle class in general consider cable channels as part and parcel of their life in this era, because they play an important role in getting them connected to the global world and to its social vicissitudes.

Mediaization Project

Prakash, a college lecturer in the Department of Personnel Management and Industrial Relations, comes from a rural setting, about 25 kilometres from Cochin, the business and commercial city in Kerala. He narrated the conflict that was going on in his house for quite sometime with regard to the television set. He says:

> The television set we have now is '86 model. It is an old model that has only a maximum of twelve channels. Parents are happy with that. They don't want to get a set having hundred channels. But I want to have one that has many more channels. The old one that we have doesn't provide foreign channels like CNN, National Geography, BBC, etc. We are yet

> to resolve that issue. [...] Anyway, now we cannot think of a life without TV. It is an important medium of entertainment. Of late, I spent lots of time before TV. I am afraid if I am getting addicted to it. I carry books from college to read them in the weekend, but not able to do anything as my time is mostly eaten up by TV. However, for parents serial operas are indispensable. They enjoy all the serials and follow up them daily. So everyday from 7 p.m. to 9.30 p.m. in the evening, television is reserved for the parents.

It is obvious that television, as an instrument of mass media, takes the form of a carefully constructed entertainment that is geared to create and permeate the ambience of consumer culture across the globe in the post-capitalist era of globalization. Samir, who comes from a rural background and is now working as a guest lecturer in higher secondary school, once told me: "My neighbour had initially decided not to have cable connection because his children were studying, but later he decided to have it. Now I see that as soon as he gets out of house, children are in front of the TV set."

Maya also narrated the case of her child stalking her because of television:

> My child who is studying in 6th standard pesters me to get some new items just because he found it very attractive in the ads. I remember him nagging me for quite sometime for the Blue Pepsi that was introduced with lots of ads during the world cup. Watching that ad, my son was making his demand every time to get one for him. But seeing its blue colour, I didn't feel good to get it.

Satellite television programmes have the capacity to seduce the consumers with its simulations, which appear to be more authentic than the original, undermining any contrast to the real by absorbing the real within itself. Consequentally, as the participants witness a television programme that is simulated, it becomes more and more difficult to distinguish the 'real' from the fake – the hyper-real – which is increasingly becoming even 'more real' than the original.

Roland Barthes (1957/1972) makes a penetrating analysis of the way in which the mythologies of advertising, fashion, popular culture and the mass media transform petit-bourgeois culture into universal 'nature'. Television programmes take the form of unifying mythologies and naturalize the contemporary society, making it appear that a historically-produced society is an expression of nature by erasing and covering over contradictions, or making them appear 'normal'. In such a situation, it becomes impossible for the consumers to distinguish between the spectacle and the real and so much so that individuals come to prefer spectacle to reality.

In this connection, Kellner's (1995) observation on the postmodern view that is associated with Baudrillard (1983) assumes significance. Baudrillard treats television as pure noise and implosion. Kellner notes:

> A black hole where all meaning and messages are absorbed in the whirlpool and kaleidoscope of radical semiurgy, of the incessant dissemination of images and information to the point of total saturation, of inertia and apathy where meaning is dissolved, where only the fascination of discrete images glow and flicker in a mediascape within which no image any longer has any discernible effects (1995, p. 233).

Baudrillard's insightful remarks point to the fact that while consumers may be critical decoders of advertisements commercial corporations, both local and global, who are not subject to any kind of democratic control and whose prime concern is profit, shape the terrain of social action and behaviour in the age of globalization.[4] This is the contemporary situation wherein Tomlinson (1991) has argued that "we are living in a global society, which is increasingly becoming a mirror of television."

Nevertheless, it has to be noted that a small percentage of 14.7 per cent of the total respondents of the quantitative investigation who still consider that satellite channels are not an essential necessity today. This considered opinion has come to prevail with them owing to reasons such as time constrain, highly expensive, promoting consumerism, lot of sexual overtones, spreading anti-Kerala values, containing negative attitudes on women, love and marriage, etc. It points to the fact that there is a small section of middle class youth, although negligible, who is well aware of the commercial and consumerist mission performed by popular media in general and TV in particular. In this connection, Reghu Dev has made a certain pertinent remarks:

> TV ads and our way of life are so much interconnected that Television has come to be a marketing technique, to sell the commodities. But now everybody becomes part of this marketing. To resist this, we need to think of counter marketing techniques. Unfortunately, nobody is bothered about it. In general, people like to flow along with the marketing currents. I like to swim the tide of life in a very peculiar manner. Although I am influenced too by this marketing wave, I am a person who would customize this and then use. For example, I don't have much belief in the cosmetics, because I don't like too much of it. I don't think that we should project ourselves externally using so much of cosmetics.

In the same way, Santhosh spoke about his 'cable experiment' that shares a contrary view with regard to the influence of television in the context of consumer culture:

> We made an experiment for sometime and connected Cable TV at home. But the moment we had cable connection, the programmes and ads in the channels were so enticing that all of us in the family seem to be interested in sitting before the TV all the time, and there was no time for any other familial activity, not even for reading and studying. I felt that my mind was getting rotten. Finally, we decided to do away with cable connection.
>
> Not only that, our youngest sister was born when three of us brothers have grown up. The changes that we notice in her make us really worried sometimes. She is exposed to a world of friends and peers who give flying kiss etc. She tends to literally imitate ads and the ambassadors of brand items. She is definitely influenced by TV shows and it is quite evident in her

> behaviour and attitudes. Now we can see tangible difference in terms of tastes, attitudes, interests, etc., in our youngest sister.

However, these opinions are made only by a negligible portion of respondents that altogether constitute only 14.7 per cent (53 respondents) of the total participants when compared to the larger number of the respondents that covered 85.3 per cent who admitted that satellite channels are an absolute necessity in the present-day world. This huge difference in the proportion of the respondents, nevertheless, reiterates the fact that TV, with its satellite network, is the medium par excellence that transmits the ideology and value system of the global trends emanated on account of the process of contemporary globalization.

Winston, a senior officer in a collaborative project meant for children in distress, initiated by Government of India shared with me that, at home, they select soaps or such items in the light of the advertisements appearing in television. Soaps like Lux, Modi etc. Each one takes according to their liking of the respective advertisement. In the case of Bobby, it is unambiguous, "I use *jeeva* soap ... I like it because of its ad in the TV; I don't know if it has any special quality than other soaps. But I want to use it. I liked the way it is advertised ... giving the feeling that it is very good ... medicinal and enhances beauty." Maximum percentage of respondents considers TV and advertisements as the main sources of information on the latest fashions, brands and models. The highest number of respondents that comprises 68.3 per cent (246 persons), however, relies on TV as the medium par excellence to provide latest trends in the market. Television advertisements do play as chief informative source of the middle class for the latest items in the market.

Maya is unambiguous in her position with regard to the influence of the mediaization of consumer culture, especially on women. She explains:

> I must tell you that of late, the concept on beauty has become a matter of serious concern for us; and the interest in it has become very rampant amidst us. It is partly because of the programmes in TV and the ads. College students, especially, find that those who appear as introducers and anchors in TV

> for variety of programmes are of their age. They are selected on account of their look and beauty. "Now if those guys can, why can't I?" could be the question that comes to their mind. The message is very clear – today what matters is appearance and look. The personality has to be exhibited in ones outfit and bodily expressions. As a result, teenagers are crazy with their 'look' and 'outfit'. That means all of them invest lot of time, money and so on to appear good and attractive.

From the perspective of the advertising industry, middle class women had to be 'seduced' to consumerism. In a paper presented at an international seminar on advertising and marketing, marketing experts Bijapurkar and Ahluwalia advised their audiences on how different consumer goods could be marketed in terms of specific semiotic codes. The experts suggested that cooking oils could be promoted in terms of purity, taste, economy and 'good housewifeliness'. On the other hand, cosmetics would have to be 'positioned' so as to "target the new, modern Indian woman promoted in advertising as westernized and independent". They claimed, "the core values of ABC as a company (and a brand) that got established as a result of its lead products, were: modern, westernized [...] women's or working women's products" (*Advertising & Marketing*, April 1982, p. 74).

"The role of advertising is to express the latent hopes and aspirations of the people and take them forward, breaking stereotypes," says the man behind the Cadbury and Perk chocolate advertisements Piyush Pandey, Creative Director, Ogilvy and Mather, Mumbai.[5] For men, as much as for women, television advertisements conferred on goods' values that resonate with their aspirations and anxieties at a time when they are struggling to consolidate their middle class status. This is the transformed ambience of middle class predicament in the age of globalization. Beck (2000) suggests that personal identity is to be understood less in terms of geography, nation, ethnicity and culture, as commonsensically maintained, but in terms of how people dream. The spectacles through which people perceive and evaluate their lives, hopes, setbacks and the present situations are made up of the prisms of possible lives which television constantly presents and celebrates. A great majority of the participants (80.8%) do think that commercial advertisements and other propaganda events have changed the dressing pattern of our young boys and girls. Dress code and pattern are significant in cultural studies that they are integrally connected to the definition of a tradition and culture. The prime media, which disseminates consumer culture, functions as agent of change in the dressing pattern of a land, in a way amounts to transformations occurring in the area of culture itself.

TV Self

While advertising *per se* was not novel to television or to economic liberalization in India, the introduction of private sponsorship of soap operas in 1982 as part of the official policy clearly demarcated the phase of the relationship between the commercial sponsorship of entertainment serials and the spread of consumerism facilitated by television among the middle classes. Although advertisements were a part of public culture before the 1980s (in the form of billboards, print advertisements and radio jingles), they became ubiquitous after Doordarshan inaugurated its sponsorship programmes. This resulted in a dramatic increase in the advertising budgets of companies in the mid-1980s, a major proportion of which was devoted to television sponsorship and commercials. Thanks to this new sponsorship scheme, major industrial companies, including prominent multinational corporations, such as Nestle, Brooke Bond and Hindustan Unilever, became important agents in the production of entertainment serials.

Serials telecast on the TV channels play great role in this 'seductive' enterprise of trapping individuals in a universe of simulacra and endow with a new form of subjectivity that can be called 'TV self,' wherein they get fully drowned into the plethora of consumer culture. In many middle class households, it has become a routine programme that the members of the family, particularly the womenfolk, regularly watch certain shows and events; there are fans for various serial operas and stars who possess an often incredible expertise and knowledge of the subjects of their fascination; people do model their behaviour, style and attitudes on television images. This is the detour through which television is playing a very significant role in managing consumer desires and demands.

The following inventory of advertisements in a single episode of a serial programme that was considered as the most popular in Malayalam channels lists the products advertised. The target audience for the advertisements may be surmised from the kinds of products advertised. This was the 303rd episode of *Sthrijanmam* (Life of Woman) featured in Soorya Channel at the prime time 7.30 p.m. to 8.00 p.m. in the evening. The telecast of the episode in a way contained four sections distinctly marked by the flow of advertisements. It is interesting to note that each section begins with a few advertisements. On the whole, it looked like telecasting a chain of advertisements with intermittent short parts lasting for five to eight minutes from a serialized novel illustrated in a popular weekly *Malayala Manorama Azhchappathippu* (Malayala Manorama Weekly) that is competing with other similar weeklies to get the largest middle class women audience. It is not surprising then that the major section of audience for the serial is also comprised of middle class women.

Part 1: Introducing the title of the serial and the details of the artists behind the production of the serial, followed by the announcement of the sponsors. First part of the serial is shown for about 10 minutes. The advertised items are:

1. Chacolas Fairness Oil the principal sponsor of the serial, in association with the following products:
2. Kaveri Fairness Cream
3. Gold Winner Sunflower Oil
4. Parris Coffee Bite
5. Poppy Umbrella
6. Yamaha Libero (Bike)
7. Jeyalakshmi Silks (Sarees)

Part 2: At about 7.12 p.m., having a major commercial break, wherein there is a flood of advertisements for about more than five minutes:

8. Chacolas Fairness Oil – featuring beautiful girls with long hair; focusing middle class women (repeat)

9. Jeyalskshmi Silks – teen-aged girls in a wedding setting; focusing women, middle class and above (repeat)
10. Goldwinner Sunflower Oil – featuring group of women, as daughter-in-law capturing appreciation from mother-in-law in the company of friends; targeting women (repeat)
11. Lux Soap – background voice of a young lady as of a fairy tale; Rs 1.50 less offer; targeting middle class youngsters
12. Parris Coffee Bite – featuring a young family; targeting middle class (repeat)
13. Poppy Umbrella – beautiful children in a flashy dance setting in rain; focusing children (repeat)
14. Close Up Lemon Mint (toothpaste) – featuring middle-aged uncle and a young handsome boy, with the slogan enabling to come closer and 'attract girls'; focusing young boys and girls
15. Odonil Bathroom Freshener – featuring a housewife and son; targeting housewives, middle class and above
16. Kaveri Fairness Cream – featuring beautiful girls and a boy with the striking message 'what a change'; targeting young girls
17. Gems Cookies – featuring a middle aged uncle and children, focusing children
18. Santoor Powder – featuring a beautiful girl, targeting youngsters
19. Mortein Mosquito Coil – featuring a mother and son in the background of an exhortation against malaria, targeting the middle class
20. Stay Free Napkin Pad – featuring beautiful girls and their young, handsome dance master, focusing young girls
21. Bhima Gold – featuring a group of beautiful girls along with a handsome man in the background of a love scene; targeting young girls
22. Nerolac Paint – featuring cine artist Mohan Lal; focusing middle class and above
23. Onida Home Theatre – featuring a young family, focusing upper class

24. Junior Horlicks – featuring a pretty young mother and her son; focusing middle class mothers
25. Mr Bean Coffee Powder – featuring young lady and a man with a cartoon song as prelude; targeting youth
26. Dettol – featuring a young middle class house wife; targeting middle class

Part 3: It is now 7.18 p.m and the episode is continued for six minutes and by 7.25 p.m. it stops for another commercial break for a set of advertisements. The advertisements were the following:

27. Yamaha Libero – featuring young handsome man; targeting young men; middle class and above
28. Lotto Jackpot – fortune lotto; 'in order that your dream come true' is the slogan; targeting the middle class
29. Khaitan Fan – featuring middle class family; targeting the middle class
30. Mr Bean coffee powder (repeat)
31. Boost – featuring a boy called Sachin in an atmosphere of a group of children playing cricket as the ideal child (bringing to memory Sachin Tendulkar, India's premier cricket player) along with a group of students looking at him proudly; focusing the middle class
32. Santoor Powder (repeat)
33. Goldwinner Oil (repeat)
34. Milkman Dairy – featuring young couple in a family setting; aiming at the middle class
35. Kannan Devan Tea – offering a Medimix Soap free for one kg. packet; aiming at the middle class
36. Santro Xing Car – featuring the Bollywood actor Sharukh Khan and a Japanese man and woman. The actor finally wins over the lady along with the car; targeting upper middle class
37. Mortein Mosquito Coil (repeat)
38. Surf Excel – featuring young couple; for the middle class

Part 4: It is nearing 7.30 p.m., surprisingly the episode continued for about another three minutes or so and at the end the sponsors' titles are announced again.

Thus, half an hour programme on television contained as many as 38 advertisements, which advertise a wide range of consumer products. The episode in a way would appear to be a chain of advertisements linked together by a few sequential frames of a popular story appeared in a periodical consumed by the same audience with great enthusiasm and involvement. As a result, commodities such as cosmetics and packaged foods, deemed luxuries in the late 1970s, etc., have become 'essentials and necessities' of the contemporary age. It becomes evident that the spread of consumer culture in the age of globalization is inextricably related to the success of television serials, which are actually locales for advertisements. In a world where consumer goods and services are multiplying by minute, the unique selling point has become the unique advertising point. As a result, the role of advertising agencies also expanded. In addition to producing and placing slots on television, some advertising agencies have also located sponsors who would finance the production of serials.

Since companies sponsored only those serials with the potential to draw large audiences, serial producers made every effort to get high ratings in order to attract and keep their sponsors. And sponsors, for their part, raced to get airtime on the most popular serials to ensure that they would reach the maximum number of viewers and/or potential consumers. Hence, the sponsorship story in a way reveals the nexus between multinational capital, the Indian state, the advertising industry and mainly the middle class audience primed to plunge into consumer culture.

Quantitative data revealed that 67.5 per cent of the participants believe that Kerala women in general are influenced by the lifestyle and notions of beauty propagated by the commercial advertisements and related spectacles. Advertising can be seen as providing some functional equivalents of myth, as in the case of many other narratives in the television. Like myths, advertisements frequently tend to resolve social contradictions, provide models of identity, and celebrate the existing social order. Barthes (1957/1972) noticed that advertising provided a repertoire of contemporary mythologies and advertisements contribute to identity formation in contemporary society. Kellner (1995), in analysing the advertisements on Marlboro cigarettes, showed that even the static images of advertising contain subject positions and models for identification that are heavily coded ideologically. The symbolic images in advertising attempt to create an association between the product offered and socially desirable and meaningful traits. In other words, advertisements form textual systems with basic components, which are interrelated in such a way that positively position the product. advertisements become social texts, which respond to key developments during the period in which they appear. Thus, Kellner submits:

> Advertising provides a utopian image of a new, more attractive, more successful, more prestigious "you" through purchase of certain goods. Advertising magically offers self-transformation; and a new identity, associating changes in consumer behaviour, fashion, and taught to identify with values, role models, and social behaviour through advertising [...] Advertising sells its products and view of the world through images, rhetoric, slogans, and their juxtaposition in ads to which tremendous artistic resources, psychological research, and marketing strategies are devoted. These ads express and reinforce dominant images of gender and position men and women to assume highly specific subject positions (1995, p. 251).

Ad-images in the ambience of consumer culture are the carriers for shaping the middle class subject positions and choices. Hence, it requires skill as to how to read images critically and unpack the relations between images, texts, social trends and products. Advertising is as concerned with selling lifestyles and socially desirable identities, which are associated with their products, as with selling the product themselves. Advertisers use the symbolic constructs with which the consumer is induced to pick a particular product amidst an array of similar products. However, it is interesting to note that the largest section who aired this opinion is the middle class women belonging to the age group of 15–30. Fifty-four out of the total 92 females comprising 52 per cent were affirmative on the opinion that advertisements do influence and condition the lifestyle and personality of the middle class women.

Figure 5.1

Reasons for women being influenced by advertisements or fashion shows

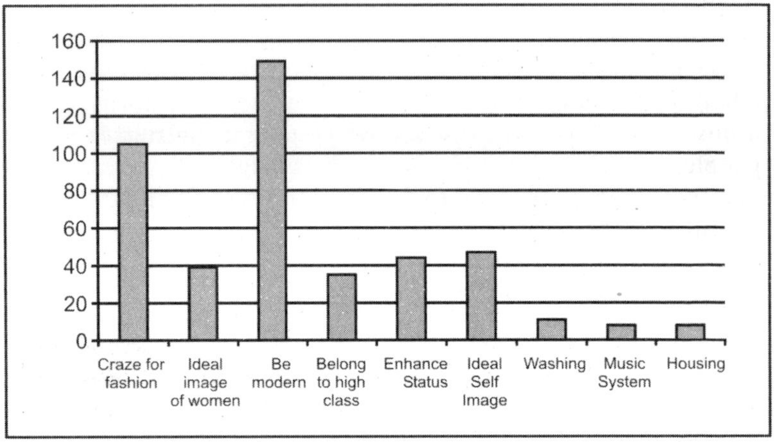

As Figure 5.1 reveals, the major reasons that the participants observe as motivating factors for women being influenced by the seductions of commercial advertisements and fashion shows are: (1) their craze to be fashionable, (2) commercial advertisements and fashion shows portraying ideal and perfect image of women, (3) as part of being modern, (4) to belong to the high class, (5) to enhance prestige and status, and (6) commercial advertisements and fashion shows project ideal self-image. Among these, 'being modern' and 'craze to be fashionable' are the reasons for which the highest proportion of participants opts for. This is rather a high percentage that constitutes 61.3 per cent of the participants who believe that women who are influenced think that it is a part of their struggle and earnestness to be modern that they look up to the commercial advertisements and other such enticing spectacles.

Global advertising sector functions as the key technology for the worldwide dissemination of creative and culturally well-chosen ideas of consumer agency. It becomes very evident that television with its cable network remains the central vehicle for international advertising in both of its multi-local and global branding forms. Television's organizational forms and programming strategies are heavily structured by the advertising industry (Barker, 1997). In this fashion, television has come to occupy the central stage in the production and reproduction of value-added commodity signs centred on the use of visual imagery.[6] In short, television renders a "market-identity as consumer in the society of the spectacle; a galaxy of hyper-fibrillated moods [...] traumatized serial being" (Kroker and Cook, 1986, p. 274). In the last instance, consumerism arouses desires which distort economic priorities and lure people into artificial consumption patterns.

The greatest fear of critics of trans-national television was that Indian culture would be 'homogenized' or, more specifically, 'Americanized' (Morley and Robins, 1995; Gupta and Ferguson, 1997). But we noticed that the plethora of channels, ranging from CNN to the BBC World Service, Star, Zee and the regional channels targeted at India's diverse linguistic groups, points to a more complex scenario. In some ways, it seemed as if cultural production had been deterritorialized as a result of trans-national satellite television. Morley and Robins' description of the reconfiguration of space in the Europe of the 1990s resonates with the experience of the middle class in Kerala:

> We are seeing the restructuring of information and image spaces and the production of new communications geography, characterized by global networks and an international space of information flows. [...] Our senses of space and place are all being significantly reconfigured [...] increasingly we must think in terms of communications and transport networks and of the symbolic boundaries of language and culture – the 'spaces of transmission' defined by satellite footprints or radio signals – as providing the crucial, and permeable, boundaries of our age" (1995, p. 1).

Globalization has indubitably increased opportunities for the movement of people, goods, business and services, to operate in markets beyond national borders. They occur in and through the growing disjuncture which constitute a model of global cultural flow. First, it occurs through people, machinery, money, images and ideas and then follows increasingly via non-isomorphic paths. However, at all periods in human history, there has been some disjuncture in the flows of these elements, but the sheer speed, scale and volume of each of these flows are unprecedented to the extent that the disjuncture has become central to the politics of global culture. Luke (1995) points to the virtual, hyper-real nature of what he depicts as the new 'global territories,' which fuse the local and the global. In other words, globalization has spawned a 'placeless' sense of the real, one based on simulation. Appadurai (1996a) aptly described this as deterritorialization of money, commodities and persons, ceaselessly chasing each other around the world resulting in the near 'end of geography'. Distances do not matter any more, although the idea of a geophysical border has increasingly become difficult to sustain in the 'real world'. Massey (1994) observes that under globalization, a new sense of place and culture has developed as opposed to the more closed and introverted sense of place and culture of the past.

Nevertheless, the time-space changes are not uniformly experienced across the globe. Some regions of the globe are more deeply implicated in global processes than others, and some are more deeply integrated into the global order than others. Within nation-states, some communities are tightly enmeshed in global networks, while others are totally excluded by them. And, even within the same street, some households are more deeply embedded in global processes than others.

Gendered Positions

The consequences of satellite television for the reconstitution of the notions of middle class womanhood and the reconfiguration of gender identity in this climate of consumer culture will have to be examined separately. It has been observed that television is an important source of social connectedness especially for middle class women and it has become an integral part of their everyday lives so much so that they even arrange their daily chores around their favourite programmes. A majority of Doordarshan's women-oriented programmes are focused on middle class families and their struggles to acquire or maintain upward mobility and middle class respectability. Mankekar (1999) has observed that with a few exceptions, Doordarshan's images of Indian womanhood were almost entirely focused on middle class.

Reghu Dev is the eldest and the only son of a higher middle class family with three children. He struggles rather unsuccessfully to assume the role of head of his family in the wake of the demise of his father some years ago. Albeit having crossed 25 years of age, he is yet to complete his postgraduation and currently engaged in some part-time job as sales executive. His mother is working in the Electricity Board. He has two younger sisters. One of them is a medical transcriptionist after her M.Sc. in Zoology and the youngest one is doing her Bachelor degree in Law. Speaking about his mother and sisters, he made the following comment:

> I like watching cable TV. I want to see HBO, CNN, ESPN, and National Geography, etc. But from 6 p.m. to 10 p.m., I have no access to these channels. My mother and sisters get engrossed in soap operas. I just don't like these programmes; because they make people stupid and brain wash them.

Reghu Dev's case indicates how 'sacred' soap operas have become especially for middle class women. Anil also faced a similar predicament. He says: "[...] whatever be the case, from 7 p.m. to 9.30 p.m., television is reserved for my mother. She is so fond of tele-serials. She sits through all of them moving from one to the other." Marketing strategies targeting women viewers/consumers created subject positions that were marked as much by class as by gender; most frequently through the category of "housewife," which is further categorized into "traditional housewives" and "modern housewives" (Miller, 1995). The market segmentation strategy followed for Procter and Gamble's Ariel detergent was typical of the ways women viewers were categorized as consumers in terms of their class positions (*Advertising & Marketing*, April 1992, p. 74). Marketing strategy for packaged foods segmented its target audience in terms of a 'typology of housewives' depending on how they used modern convenient foods: 'traditional housewives', 'nutrition-conscious housewives', and 'convenience seekers' (MARG, from the *Economic Times*, July 8, 1992).

Stereotypes and generalizations in advertisements confine women to the traditional role of a mother, or beauty or sex symbol, and these do not represent women's diversity. The tentacles of consumer culture spread through advertisements and related spectacles continue to objectify women, and place stress on their appearance, thus devaluing their innate worth. Irigaray (1985) makes an illuminating comment that women viewers positioned themselves as commodities because they were 'sold' to sponsors as well as to advertisers as prospective consumers. Irigaray claims ironically using Levi-Straus's model of the 'exchange' of women, "the economy of exchange of desire is man's business" (p. 177).

The advertising discourses position women viewers as subjects who 'consumed' not only the commodities being advertised, but also notions of modern Indian womanhood constructed through semiotic chains of images and desires. Consumer culture by creating a domain of commodity aesthetics built on seductive values of commodities, constructs women's subjectivities through the constitution of their desires. Women viewers seem to be construed as both objects and subjects of consumption through their location in the circuit of exchange and their fetishization in terms of specific commodified values. Media misrepresentation of women in advertisements has created plenty of stereotypical representations of women. In one such common stereotype, female body is used differently in comparison to male body in advertisements. Women are often shown in a sexual or vulnerable position in order to sell the product, whether it is an advertisement for shaving cream or alcoholic beverage. Ordinary women tend to be less satisfied with their own attractiveness when they watch advertisements showing beautiful female models.

Body Matters

Discourse on advertising frequently hinged on the objectification of the female body. As in United States[7], many Indian advertisements segmented the female body into hair, face, legs, breasts and so on. Several feminist critics of television have commented on this sexual objectification of women. For instance, Krishnan and Dighe describe how in many advertisements, "the caressing movements of the camera sweeping over women's bodies engage the male viewer as object" (1990, p. 90). Hence, the questions about the social construction and disciplining of women's bodies particularly have been central to the contemporary feminist theory. The consumer culture of the recent times have made it possible for the increasing visibility of the body, in both popular culture and media, through sexed representation and body-transformative practices, and this has caught the focus of academic debate.[8]

It is not surprising, then, that a large number of participants aired that TV do influence the viewer's notions of the body. Seventy-three per cent comprising 263 participants are aware of the fact that television does make an impact on their concept of body. All categories of respondents in terms of variables such as age, sex, religion and income seem to be unanimous in this perception and the variation according to different indicators was found to be insignificant. Mankekar (1999) made an ethnographic study on the effect of television on Indian womanhood. She has observed that the widespread reach of television and the launching of commercial programmes titillated the consumerist desires of viewing subjects by introducing them to a range of goods that promised to make their lives more modern, more exciting, more middle class (pp. 75–79). In fact, women's subjectivities are constructed through the constitution of their desires filliped by carefully organized tele-visual world of consumer culture. In a way, this also informs us about the consequences of transnational capital and the media for the reconfiguration of gender identity.

Related to this idea, the process of reconfiguring gender identity is the manner in which spread of consumer culture affects the position and status of women in middle class families. Although the practice of demanding dowry existed even before liberalization and the advent of commercials on television, women's groups, social scientists and journalists, all believe that television commercials whetted people's appetites for such consumer durables as washing machines, expensive kitchen appliances, and, most importantly, colour television sets. Whereas in earlier times, dowry demands took the form of cash, jewellery, and in some cases, vehicles, recent dowry demands consist of consumer durables that had become available only after liberalization (Mankekar, 1999, p. 99). In this context, Angelo shared with me the unethical and unconstitutional aspect involved in certain advertisements. He cited the case of the advertisements for 'Santro Plus' (Zip Plus), "It read something like this: 'Are you happy that you are going to give away your girl to somebody? You can offer a wonderful gift – something she adores ...' This definitely endorses dowry and it is against Indian constitution and culture ... but still it is being promoted and marketed."

It becomes unambiguously evident that youth and middle class are the esteemed beneficiaries and advocates of the consumer culture that is ubiquitous in the globalized age. Among all the participants, only 77.2 per cent believe that in terms of the income class it is the middle class which is mostly influenced and conditioned by the advertisements and other publicity events (Figure 5.2).

In the same manner, a thumbing majority of 84.2 per cent of the respondents consider that it is the youth as a category who is influenced most by the advertisements and publicity events (Figure 5.3).

Figure 5.2

Income class category most influenced by advertisements and similar spectacles

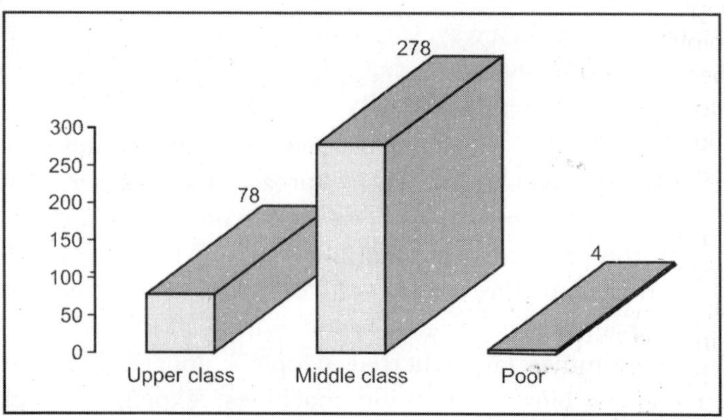

Figure 5.3

Age group most influenced by advertisements and publicity shows

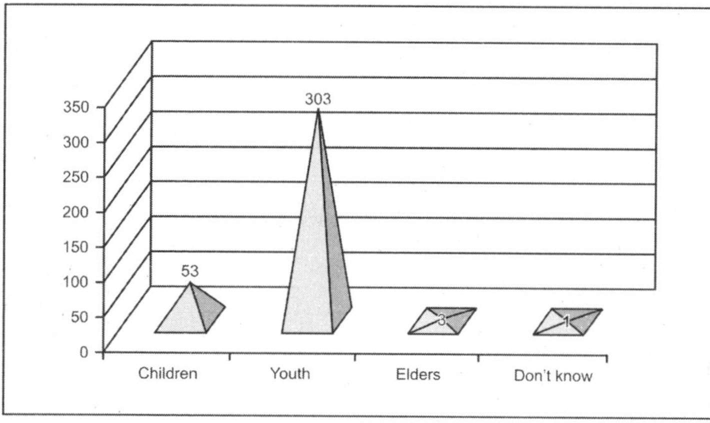

Referring to an anecdote from his own life, Seby confirmed this fact about the middle class youth. When I met Seby, he was a postgraduate student doing Personnel Management. He was very popular in the college with his talents in fast and brisk dance numbers that are trendy in the college campus these days. Later, in the final year of his college, he was elected as the Arts Club Secretary. In his words:

> Advertisements influence teenagers greatly. In my own case, I got really crazy to get a bike when I was doing plus two. All my friends had bikes. I used to feel terribly bad without a bike when I was with my friends. Finally I went for the most popular bike – Suzuki Shogun. It had a very good look; and the colour of the stickers was very attractive. But much more than these, amidst teenagers, its possession brought high status. It was part of my status too. That time all my friends considered bikes very important. I found that all those who owned bikes had good friends. I wanted the company of my friends too.

It is observed that advertisements in cable channels along with sports spectacles, beauty pageants and rock concerts, not only target the generation who mostly identifies with variety of brand images, but also contribute to a fetishization of youthful, sporty body which has made weight-loss programmes such a lucrative industry in western countries.[9] As a result, advertisements which target them, in fact, exhort them to break the cultural fabric of society and break its codes of values and ethics. Today's mass market and entertainment have only increased the craving for new symbols of differentiation, which advertisers have learnt only too well to target. The vast majority of the respondents comprising more than 91 per cent of the total sample were of the opinion that the advertisements and the entry of new and variety of consumer items do influence the lifestyle of young girls and boys. The middle class youth, in particular, tend to move along with the tide of globalization by succumbing to the major instruments and forces brought by it. This is the trajectory in which youth becomes a stereotype both for commercial success as well as for sexual attraction; and thus, for what appears to be happiness and success. When we look at the age-wise break-up of this data, we find that 92.4 per cent of the total number of youth themselves has shared this view. That makes 52.1 per cent of the total respondents who believed that the advertisements and the entry of new and variety of consumer items have an influence on young boys and girls (Table 5.1).

Table 5.1

Age-wise break-up of the opinion whether advertisements and the flow of goods influence youngsters

Age group	*Advertisements and flow of goods influencing youngsters*		*Total*
	Yes	*No*	
15–30	171 *(92.4%) 52.1%	14 *(7.6%) 43.8%	185 (51.4%)
31–55	140 *(90.3%) 42.7%	15 *(46.8%) 46.9%	155 (43.1%)
56–70	17 *(85%) 5.2%	3 *(15%) 9.4%	20 (5.6%)
Total	328 (100.0%)	32 (100.0%)	360 (100.0%)

*Percentage in terms of the respective age group.

Thus, this idea has substantial degree of validation from the point of view of participants themselves. Hence, it is to be highlighted that even the subjects themselves, or insiders – perceive that the enticing environment of consumer culture exerts a definite impact on the life of middle class youth. In this regard, Maya's comments express serious concern:

> I don't have a cable connection at home. As I had told you earlier, we have avoided it purposely. In fact, I like watching all the programmes in the cable channels, but I am afraid I get addicted to it. Co-sister's family also has cut the cable connection now. My niece there used to spend hours before the TV shuttling through different channels. She used to watch TV programmes late at night. She is doing her degree. Eventually, this has become a habit of her that she even had sleepless nights. Naturally, this affected her studies. *Chechi* (elder sister) always tells me that she is so much taken up by fashions and new trends in costumes and make-ups that she at times is worried about her daughter's unwarranted enthusiasm in these matters. And so, finally they were forced to remove the cable connection.

In the final analysis, this exploration has brought us to the intersection wherein we realize the interconnection between the middle class cultural fabric being redefined in conjunction with trans-national satellite television as the esteemed medium of communication, information and entertainment. Adorno (1984) has pointed to the increasing dominance of exchange value that obliterated the original use value of things. In the process, the commodity took on an ersatz or secondary use value, which Baudrillard later referred to as 'sign value'. This ethnographic narrative unambiguously reveals the fact that commercial manipulation of images of the cultural fabric of daily life, through the mediaization of the displays, performances, spectacles and advertising, demands a constant re-working of desires through images. In an environment of consumer culture, the experience of everything, from goods to culinary habits, music, television, entertainment and cinema, makes one to feel the world's geography vicariously, as a *simulacrum*. The interweaving of simulacra in daily life brings together different worlds of commodities within the same space and time. But it does so in such a way as to conceal almost perfectly any trace of origin, of the labour processes that produce them, or of the social relations implicated in their production. Hence, as Haug (1986, 1987) mentioned that consumer culture, in the wake of globalization, must not be regarded as only releasing a dominant materialism which is typical of a post capitalistic society, but it also confronts people with dream images which speak to desires, aestheticize and derealize reality.

This is how the new departmental stores and arcades are transformed to temples in which goods are worshipped as fetishes. The mass media of the twenty-first century, with the growing advertising industry and television, apparently replicate the world of commodity as 'dream worlds' and 'sign worlds' endlessly. The next chapter explores its direct effect on middle class and examines the accommodative and resistant posture employed by the middle class when engulfed by the currents of consumer culture.

Notes

1. For a detailed discussion, see Mankekar (1999, pp. 54–57); also Singhal and Rogers, 1989, pp. 66–67.
2. For example, the advertisement budget of India's biggest spender on advertising, Hindustan Uniliver, grew by 22 per cent in just one year. The advertisement expenditure of certain sectors such as consumer electronics, of special interest to the middle class, grew in 1995 by as much as 70 per cent as against a growth in sales of less than 30 per cent.
3. See S.H. Venkatramani in *The Pioneer,* March 30, 1996.
4. The rapid expansion of the consumer market is evident from the following statistics: sales of TV sets jumped from 2 million to 23.4 million between 1981 and 1990; and between 1984 and 1990, the annual sales of packaged consumer goods shot up by 220 per cent (Kulkarni, 1992, p. 45). Described by advertising industry, leaders as the "most persuasive, the most cost-effective and the quickest medium" these advertisements catered to the urban and, later, rural middle classes (A. Chatterjee, *Economic Times,* January 30, 1991, p. 4).

The early 1990s saw the increasing presence of multinational and monopoly capital on television. Most of the advertisers on television consisted either of multinational companies and their subsidiaries, such as Colgate-Palmolive, Brooke Bond, Ponds, and FSL, or major Indian corporations such as Tatas, Birlas, Modi, Godrej and TVS (Mankekar, 1999, p. 82).

5. Advertising and Marketing, April 1982, p. 74.
6. Mankekar (1999, p. 80) elucidates the marketing success story of television that launched a new era in the history of organic nexus between commercial advertising and television serials. The author illustrates the case of *Hum Log,* the serial that became the vehicle for the first time, which marketed Maggi Noodles. Maggi Noodles was thus introduced to a captive audience of more than 50 million people between 1984 and 1985, and sales rose from none in 1982 to 1,600 tonnes in 1983 and to about 5,000 tonnes in 1984. More significant, the success of Maggi Noodles made packaged foods not just acceptable but, because of their convenience and modern image, *desirable* to the middle class audience. See also Singhal and Rogers (1989) and Mitra (1995).
7. See Doane (1989) on the fetishization of the female body in US television advertisements.
8. See, for instance, Arthurs and Grimshaw edited book, titled *Women's Bodies: Discipline and Transgression,* London and New York: Cassell Publishers, 1999.
9. Debashish Mukerji, "The Great Indian Middle Class" in *The Week,* Anniversary Issue, December 30, 2001.

CHAPTER 6

Consumer Subject

In the ambience of consumer culture, popular periodicals, television, film, and other products of the culture industries help produce the fabric of everyday life; particularly for the middle class, they provide the material out of which people forge their very identities. Thus, media industry has come to dominate everyday life, serving as the ubiquitous background and often the highly seductive foreground especially of middle class attention and activity. Media and consumer culture work hand in hand to generate thought and behaviour in conformity with the belief, values and practices; they also forge the identities accordingly in the age of globalization. Therefore, it may be well postulated that the middle class desires and the political economy of consumerism are integrally linked to the prevailing media culture that has contributed substantially to the spread of consumerism among the middle class.

An important aspect of the consumer behaviour of the Indian middle class is that they now purchase certain items more in quantity and frequency; compared to their buying behaviour about two decades ago. Some of these items, which the middle class is more prone to buy, according to the order of their priority are: fashionable clothes, cosmetics, vehicles, essential and nutritional food articles and footwear. It is revealing that clothes, cosmetics and vehicles top the list of items that middle class desire is centred around. Bobby makes a general observation on this:

> Now, there is definite change in our buying habit. For instance, food items: earlier we used to get them in lot of quantity, but now we go for quality too. Lots of food items are available in the market, which are more attractive, and with better ads. [...] This creates a craving in us to experiment with newer items, models and brands. In my case, I have a special liking for clothes. I buy more clothes of late; may be because I am a student. My liking for clothes is part of my self-image. Friends should have a regard for me.

At the same time, no marked difference was noticed in general among the diverse income levels within the middle class in procuring some of the most expensive and prestigious items like four-wheeler, TV, cable network, computer, internet connection, mobile phone, etc.

Table 6.1

Income-group-wise distribution of the buying preferences for expensive consumer durables

Income class	*Expensive consumer goods*						
	Four-wheeler	*TV*	*Cable*	*Computer*	*Internet*	*Mobile*	*Total*
Lower middle (Rs 5,000–10,000)	19 *(9.8%) 27.1%	187 (96.4%) 53.9%	119 (61.3%) 48.4%	47 (24.2%) 40.5%	25 (2.9%) 35.2%	55 (28.4%) 50.0%	194
Middle middle (Rs 10,000–15,000)	29 (24.8%) 41.4%	114 (97.4%) 32.9%	87 (74.4%) 35.4%	40 (34.2%) 34.5%	27 (23.1%) 38.0%	30 (25.6%) 27.3%	117
Upper middle (Rs 15,000–20,000)	22 (44.9%) 31.4%	46 (93.9%) 13.3%	40 (81.6%) 16.3%	29 (59.2%) 25.0%	19 (38.8%) 26.8%	25 (51%) 22.7%	49
Total	70 (100%)	347 (100%)	246 (100%)	116 (100%)	71 (100%)	110 (100%)	360 (100%)

* Percentage of the income groups.

'Must Buy' Mania

There is a progressive increase in the proportion of those who possess these items from the lower income middle class to the higher income middle class. One notable exception to this pattern of increase is in the case of mobile phones. In the ownership of mobile phones, the percentage of the lower middle class is higher than that of the higher income middle class groups (Table 6.1). It is not surprising that almost all the respondents (96.4%) belonging to the triple levels of income groups possess a TV. This confirms the fact that TV is an integral component in the lives of the middle class people in the post-capitalistic era of globalization. Franklin made a pertinent observation with regard to this changed buying habit of the middle class. He describes:

> We have lots of new varieties of products now in the market. For example, apples and grapes from countries like Australia and Israel. Earlier they came only from within the country. Now many houses have cable connection too and they get trapped there. People are addicted to TV. My mother is a typical case. These new items are shown in TV advertisements. Especially when middle class people like us go for shopping, we find those attractive items in shops and are inclined to buy them even if we don't have money. We then tend to borrow money at exorbitant rates of interest from moneylenders and thus get caught up in the vicious circle of *Kadakeni* (debt trap).

Respondents recorded a number of significant changes occurring in the consumer market today from ten years back (Figure 6.1). They perceived the few changes in the market in the order of priority which facilitated the heightened buying behaviour of the middle class. The important changes are: (1) increased number of products and brands (60%); (2) more processed, packed and bottled products; (3) higher standard of quality products (49.4%); (4) better purchasing schemes and benefits (31.7%); (5) more and variety shops, selling and buying centres and delivery schemes and points (22.8%); and (6) better advertisements, means of publicity and information (22.2%).

These stated changes, which emerged in a period of about ten years, are closely related to and are the specific outcomes of consumer culture, which is a characteristic feature of post-capitalistic era of globalization.

Figure 6.1

Changes perceived in the nature of market

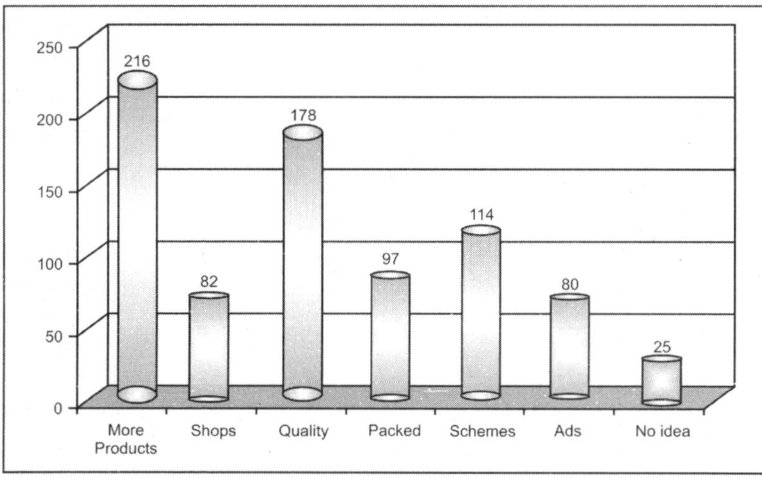

Santhosh recalled his experience of the market and a case of being trapped by the market recently:

> Market has definitely changed from what it was ten years ago. It was then need-based. Now, we are induced. We fall into the trap at times. Market gives the impression that certain items are essential for living. The other day we had an experience at home. The representatives from Eureka Forbes Vacuum Cleaner came home and demonstrated that bed and so on contain lots of dust that we inhale. We then thought that a machine of that kind is very essential for us and ultimately we opted to buy it.

The 'must buy' tendency of the contemporary middle class seems to spread like wildfire. "We want more because we see more" appears to be the kind of slogan that governs middle class consumers today. Maya has told me this with a tint of guilt, "We sometimes go for outings and tours as a family. Then I make it a point to do some extra shopping. Of late, this appears to be a more frequent affair with us. Apparently, I look forward to such trips. Definitely, these are times of extravagance." Winston, hailing from a rural setting, once spoke about a new tendency that is noticed in the food habits of his neighbours. He says, "Ours is a village, but Noodles, Macaroni etc., have become very common in our place. One reason for this is the permeating presence of advertisements. When people, especially children watch those advertisements, they are enticed." Santhosh opined that the changes in the food habits and tastes of the middle class Malayalis are common phenomena, irrespective of regional differences and it is interrelated to the general trend in the consumer habits as such. He says:

> Now I find that we use lots of packaged food because they are more convenient. For instance, my sister who is studying in 7th class likes Maggie noodles, which I had not even heard of during my schooling. Western tastes catch hold of us unawares. My brother goes for most modern Jeans, Baggies, etc. Sister also follows suit. When we noticed dangerous signals in her behaviour and attitude, we disconnected the cable connection itself.

Maya explored the ramifications and dynamics of these emerging shifts in the food habits and tastes when I posed this issue before her. She declares:

> We used to get plenty of Macaroni, Noodles and this type of food items. Husband and I liked them very much. But later, we learned that they are not good for health. So we reduced their use. But still we use them occasionally. They were not so frequent, say about fifteen years ago, as they are available now and have become so common. This spread is definitely on account of the ads and the change in lifestyle of the people. But I must tell you that I feel they have even transformed our old taste. I doubt if these new tastes go with our traditional and indigenous tastes. When we use these new items, we don't really enjoy their taste, but then we slowly develop a taste for

> them. Finally, there comes to a point when we feel that something must be wrong with us if we are not able to enjoy their taste; since several of us in and around our neighbourhood, including those who are below our status and standard, seem to like their taste. When we see the ads in TV and elsewhere, we also feel like tasting them. Then we are excited and feel like getting them for our use. When everybody else appears to be enjoying their taste, and if we alone are not able to enjoy, then we tend to feel that may be our problem.

In the same way, we find a soaring trend in the use of beverages. A very high percentage of participants perceive that the use of beverages has increased in Kerala during the past ten years. We have 93.3 per cent, constituting 336 persons, of respondents who think that there is definite increase in the consumption of soft drinks such as Coca-Cola, Pepsi, Mirinda, and Sprite. The general consumption of beverages has increased in Kerala compared to ten years ago. Samir spoke about its' pervasive nature:

> High-income group students who come from rural locality take a lot of them. They are simply taken up by ads and the attractions of the ambassadors who are heroes and heroines. Also, I have felt that it has something to do with status and prestige. When I see some of my college mates or others and the way they open the bottle and drink, we also would feel like having one. It looks as though they feel great, once they drink it. When I travel in train, I see people going with these bottles as though they are great, with high status.

Winston told me that even in their *pucca* village *pettikkada* (street vending shop), Coca-Cola was available and there were many takers for it. Franklin commented once:

> Use of Coca-Cola is connected with status and prestige. Instead of pure water, people tend to use beverages. It has become very common now for parties and marriages. They seem to think that there is *style and glamour* involved in it. It is very popular only because of ads. Ordinary people feel that it is something great when the so-called big heroes appear as ambassadors of these products and use it.

On the other hand, we must also say that even if the general consumption of these products which are considered typical commodities that proclaim the pervasive nature of consumer culture and symbolize it, a high proportion of the middle class in a way maintains due discretion in the use of it. However, the pertinent question is with regard to the reason for this perceived discretion. Is it something related to any value or ideology, or merely utilitarian and functional?

As a matter of fact, many use beverages and not other ordinary and indigenous drinks, mainly because they consider this beverages more healthy (51.8%), convenient to carry during travel (47.4%) and so on. First of all, questions can be raised regarding the reasons that they put forward for their preference in choosing beverages, since a good percentage of participants (49.1%) seem not to use them at all. Secondly, this points to the fact that the advertisements and other publicity devices on these drinks have succeeded in attracting at least a sizeable portion of the middle class and other sections of people as potential consumers. The advertisements go even to the extent of injecting false information on a vital aspect such as health.

Homo Consumers

In this context, a question may be asked whether thirst-refreshment is merely a physiological effect, or, it is a psychological problem because of the knowledge that a particular product is quality-approved by a laboratory and clinically tested. Knowledge, especially produced in laboratory, is treated as powerful. Dipankar Gupta (2000) submits that social, economic and political power is etched into lab technologies and tests. He is of the opinion that mass extraction and synthesis of plant compounds occur in reaction to consumer demand. On this question, Bobby had the following to say:

> If available, I like to drink bottled drinks. But I have a feeling that they are not good for health; hence my interest in them has declined of late. But there is a general tendency today that it is preferable and prestigious to drink these beverages. The other day I found a middle-aged man drinking Cola in a petty teashop, seems he is doing a great thing. This tendency has

become widespread. Now people tend to drink Cola and Pepsi instead of tea and coffee. Once I saw in a bank that all the staff drinking Pepsi in the evening. I have a feeling that we have to resist this tendency; I liked the idea of tender coconut revolution. In Changanacherry, where I come from, it clicked.

There is yet another aspect to be highlighted in this regard. An income-wise tabulation of this data revealed that out of the 31.7 per cent of the respondents who prefer to consume beverages, the highest proportion that comprises 62.3 per cent of the total comes from the lower-middle class group.

Table 6.2

Respondents' preference for beverages in terms of income class

Income class	*Preferred beverages*		*Total*
	Yes	*No*	
Lower-middle (Rs 5,000–10,000)	71 **(36.6%) 62.3%	123 (63.4%) 50.0%	194 53.9%
Middle-middle (Rs 10,000–15,000)	31 (26.5%) 27.2%	86 (73.5%) 35.0%	117 32.5%
Upper-middle (Rs 15,000–20,000)	12 (24.5%) 10.5%	37 (75.5%) 15.0%	49 13.6%
Total	114 100.0%	246 100.0%	360 100.0%

**Percentages given in parentheses show the frequency within the respective group.

The percentage of the lower-middle class seems to be very high compared to the proportion of the other two income groups. Does this point to the fact that it is the lower middle class people who are in the front stage of actors aspiring to imbibe the value systems of status and prestige and norms of identity generated and transmitted vociferously by channels of globalization? The lower-middle class, being situated in between the poor and the upper class and who remain at the back seat of the middle class in general want to strive hard to keep up their status and show that they are not so behind in the social ladder in terms of class. However, in this regard, no significant difference is shown either between the different age groups or sex. This means that the variables such as age and sex do not seem to affect the preference for beverages and that it is primarily income status that determines the attitude and behaviour of the middle class in terms of their buying habit and thereby imbibing the value system of the present-day consumer culture.

Table 6.3

Respondents' preference for beverages in terms of age group

Age group	*Preferred beverages*		*Total*
	Yes	*No*	
15–30	60 **(32.4%) 52.6%	125 (67.6%) 50.8%	185 51.4%
31–55	51 (32.9%) 44.7%	104 (67.1%) 42.3%	155 43.1%
56–70	3 (15%) 2.6%	17 (85%) 6.9%	20 5.6%
Total	114 100.0%	246 100.0%	360 100.0%

**Percentages given in parentheses show the frequency within the respective group.

Coming to those participants who choose not to use beverages, as Bobby stated, the prime reason is again health grounds as they bear a belief that soft drinks are unhealthy compared to water and other ordinary local drinks. So, the attitude and behaviour of the middle class regarding the use of beverages seem to be not necessarily motivated by a principle or ideology. Nevertheless, there is a minority group who resist it partly on account of their articulated ideology too. Samir for instance, belongs to this group. He declares:

> Somehow I was not fascinated by these multinational beverages like Coca-Cola. And as and when I came to know more about such beverages, I decided not to take it. Not because they are *Videshi* (foreign) products, or I am a person who likes to lead a *Swadhesi* (of local, indigenous) lifestyle. But I have come to known about the ill-effects, and heard lots of talks about them. They bring cultural, economic and even environmental problems with them. The nature cure method

also has conducted lots of experiments and I have heard from the nature cure doctors about the bad effects produced by these beverages.

Respondents, who belong to the genre of Samir, shared some reasons for their apparent objection to beverages that are closely linked to the prevailing consumer culture in the age of globalization (Figure 6.2).

Figure 6.2

Reasons for not consuming beverages

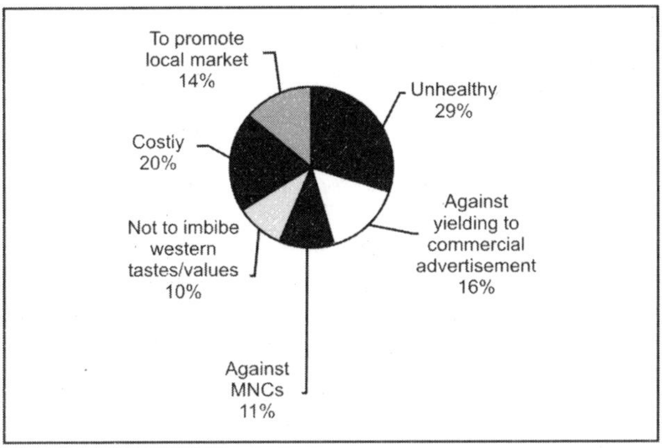

The reasons included the following: 'to resist the undue influence of advertisements and other propaganda spectacles'; 'not to yield to the multinational strategies of commercial operations'; 'to be aware of the danger of imbibing western values and tastes'; and 'the need to promote local markets'. However, only a very thin percentage of respondents remarked on such plausible propositions; for the larger proportion, health concern still remained the main reason that factored in avoiding the consumption of beverages. Hence, the disposition of the respondents in general seems to suggest that utility and function rather than value or ideology mostly determine the attitude of the middle class to consumer culture. In other words, the middle class, by and large, seems to operate in an accommodative and integrationist framework to the consumerist changes facilitated by the phenomenon of globalization. Winston was more vocal about the ill-effects of beverages:

> I think multinational companies who manufacture these beverages in our land have to be packed off. They make us stupid and exploit us; their production cost is so cheap, but they take exorbitant price from us and simultaneously cheating us with all kinds of ads and publicity. Thirdly, our traditional products and items are rated as third rate and their market is reduced so much. If we use tender coconut and fresh juice, that will benefit our farmers and good for our health too.
>
> It has also something to do with status. People think that their worth goes up if others see them drinking these beverages, instead of tender coconuts. And they sell this in a handy form. My brother is a fan of Coca-Cola. Although I know this, still I might get one of this for occasions such as in his birthday. However, they make the ads very attractive and glamorous with great heroes and ambassadors. People are attracted by these advertisements too.

The widespread use of beverages is an instance par excellence that confirms the perception of Cvetkovich and Kellner (1997) that the resultant 'electronic reach' of Hollywood, McDonald, Coca-Cola, Nike, Adidas, etc., is a distinguished trend of the contemporary world resulting in the spread of a 'new world culture'. Cvetkovich and Kellner observe: "The consumer society, with its panorama of goods and services; trans-national forms of architecture and design; and a wide range of products and social forms is traversing national boundaries and becoming part of a new world culture" (1997, p. 7).

It is evident that the influence of consumer culture not only operates on a large scale, but also penetrates "the significant, the routine and the most intimate aspects of life" so much so that *Homo sapiens* are now transformed into *Homo consumers*. However, there are marked differences in the added values imputed to the commodities in the country of origin and management and in other satellite consuming countries. This is the reason why the term 'consumer culture' points to the ways in which consumption ceases to be a simple appropriation of utilities or use values, and is transferred to a realm of consumption of signs and images, which continuously reshape the cultural or symbolic aspect of the commodity. As a result, the culture of the consumer society transforms itself to a vast floating complex of fragmentary signs and images, which produces an endless sign-play that destabilizes long-held symbolic meanings and cultural order. Referring to this aspect of consumer culture, Maya made a pertinent comment:

> This has also something to do with status symbol. I think, now, we have special fascination for the West that we want to imitate western styles in our basic life-situations like food, dress, etc. In my case when I was younger, the West was something like what I could only dream about, especially when we read about the progress they make and when we see the lifestyle of our own people who come back from there. It was certainly a big dream for us; I thought we can lead an affluent life there [...] 'must be a very beautiful place to live in' such kind of feelings. But later these whims and fancies got reduced; and now I don't entertain these thoughts. Perhaps now, whatever we desire is available within our reach; all those attractions, which haunted my youthful dreams, can be realized here; and now anything and everything is available to us in our own place.

Maya seems to be pointing to the debate on the issue of unidirectional cultural flow that is built in the globalization project. It entails more than just the simple spread of American or Western cultural goods, more than the development of a global taste for McDonald's, Levis, Coca-Cola and the like. At a deeper level, it involves the worldwide installation of a Western version of basic social-cultural reality, particularly, the West's epistemological and ontological theories, its values, ethical systems, approaches to rationality, technical and scientific worldview, politics, culture and so on. In other words, consumer culture entails the dissemination of all facets of the West's way of being. In this sense, Maya seems to be referring to the 'westoxication' tendency about which Gupta (2000) speaks.[1] According to Gupta, westoxication "is about superficial consumerist display of commodities and fads produced in the West" and it is usually mistaken for westernization (2000, p. 11). The trajectory of westoxication, in fact, constitutes the 'localization' de tour of consumer culture, wherein the two-way process of 'universalization of particularism' as well as 'particularization of universalism' occurs. It is marked by the development of what King (1990) aptly termed 'global cities' as local sites of global interaction; there is a huge increase in the flows of commodities and cultural products, and finally the world-wide spread of Western-style consumerism. All this, in a way, points to the over arching "social process in which the constraints of geography on social and cultural arrangements recede and people become increasingly aware that they are receding" (Waters, 1995, p. 3). We learn that people are virtually influenced by the global, but this is interpreted locally and local transformations are as much a part of consumer culture as the lateral extension of social connections across time and space.

Cultural Disembedding

Thus, we are at the heart of the issue that consumer culture is basically geared to radically pull culture apart from places, and dislodge it from particular locales. As revealed in the empirical exploration, the signs of this disembedding are the ubiquitous presence and demand for the cultural objects (food, drinks, appliances and so forth) and their circulation through ever-expanding networks. Simultaneously, images too are drifting easily across the globe, allowing an increase in the number of middle class to participate in the imagined realities of other cultures. Hence, the consumption tendencies, practices and the lifestyle of the middle class point towards the fact that our society has started reflecting a world of culture in motion.

Culture in contemporary environment has to be understood as a product of a continuous interplay between its universalistic aspects and its particularistic reproduction. As Appadurai (1999, p. 231) argues much of the work on globalization has been framed in terms of the dialectic between 'the global' and 'the local'. The cultural landscapes in the 1990s saw a complex of initiatives centred on new narratives of consumption and desire, wherein the new cultural space is criss-crossed by a fluidity of national, regional and global cultural styles mediated by the recognition of a new agent 'the consumer-subject'.

One way of approaching global culture is in terms of Schiller's (1985) influential macro-economic domination theory, which reflects that cultural imperialism, as well as the anticipated cultural homogenization arising from it, results from multinational capitalism and its insatiable drive for new markets and maximum profits. It is undeniable that new communicational technologies are shrinking the world and, as Cvetkovich and Kellner (1997, p. 3) put it, there is a "dramatic perpetration of global forces into every realm of life in every region of the world." Beck talks of cultural 'de-location' and 're-location' and concludes that "[...] local cultures can no longer be justified, shaped and renewed in seclusion from the rest of the world [...] there is a compulsion to re-locate de-traditionalized traditions within a global context of exchange dialogue and conflict" (2000, p. 47).

The quantitative data illuminates us further when we analyse it in relation to the income class. It is again the lower-middle class group that tops in the percentage among the triple income categories in the increased purchase of all these items. We find a marked difference in the percentage of the first two income levels, specifically the lower-middle and middle-middle and the upper-middle age group (Table 6.4). The purchasing capability of the upper-middle class remained more or less steady before and after the advent of the contemporary market trends.

Table 6.4

Income-wise distribution of the items of which the buying has increased

Income class	*Food*	*Nutrition*	*Fashionable clothes*	*Cosmetics*	*Vehicles*
Lower-middle (Rs 5,000–10,000)	55 52.4%	51 52.6%	92 54.8%	65 46.4%	78 56.1%
Middle-middle (Rs 10,000–15,000)	35 33.3%	26 26.8%	53 31.5%	50 35.7%	45 32.4%
Upper-middle (Rs 15,000–20,000)	15 14.3%	20 20.6%	23 13.7%	25 17.9%	16 11.5%
Total	105 100.0%	97 100.0%	168 100.0%	140 100.0%	139 100.0%

But, the existing buying capacity of the lower-middle class and the middle-middle class would not suffice to meet the additional needs and aspirations generated by the seductive value enhancement injected in the consumer products and thus to cope with the general buying-inducing atmosphere of consumer culture. A further analysis of the data for which considerable increase in buying has occurred in relation to the sex variable, reveals an interesting feature. Whereas males dominate the market of buying of fashionable clothes and vehicles, it is females who dominate the buying of cosmetics.

Table 6.5

Sex-wise distribution of three major items whose buying has increased

Sex	*Fashionable clothes*	*Cosmetics*	*Vehicles*	*Total*
Male	105 **(47.1%) 62.5%	73 (32.8%) 52.1%	89 (40%) 64.0%	223
Female	63 (46%) 37.5%	67 (49%) 47.9%	50 (36.5%) 36.0%	137
Total	168 100.0%	140 100.0%	139 100.0%	360

** Percentages given in parentheses show the frequency within the respective sex group.

The eradication of cultural differences seems to be the advantage of Western capitalism and to the detriment of both culturally and economically 'colonized' locale. Schiller (1976, 1985, 1996) submits that Western countries dominate economic and technological resource, so much so that the developing world is doomed to remain at the margins of the global economy. Multinational corporations control the global market and exploit cheap labour and resources wherever they can be located. The cultural homogeneity thesis boils down to a fear that everywhere it is, at least culturally, becoming similar and that local and national cultures are being subsumed by a shallow, inauthentic and synthetic global culture based on the economic domination of the West and the products of the powerful trans-national media corporations. The fear is that, world wide, local cultural difference is being attacked and eroded by mass-produced Western goods (James, 1993). For example, 'Coca-colization' is interpreted by some as a recolonization of the non-Western world by fetishized Western goods carrying with them hugely invasive connotations of Western success and affluence

(Hannerez, 1990). A debate with regard to the many issues associated with the enormous shifts under way in India, would make it clear that the connection between public culture and global cultural flows was at the heart of the matter. Many of the changes we could see are the result of the changes in global capital and also in the cultural flows that it appeared to encourage. Thus, the public sphere also looked like a promising entry into the local reception and transformation of global cultural flows.

This situation would naturally result in two things: first, it would prompt the border categories of lower-middle and middle-middle groups to yield the pervading buying sentiments of the emerging market. Secondly, the seductive value elevation of the commodities in the context of globalization may compel them to find ways and means to possess those prestigious items and services and thus to satisfy the created urge for conspicuous consumption. Maya had something specific to speak about it.

> I find that the use of Maggie Noodles has become so common that even lower middle class people buy them as frequently as the upper middle class or rich people. When I was working in General Hospital, I have seen that even the last grade staff who lived on loans and borrowings used to get these special items. When I heard about their food pattern and style, I was astonished. They say that our children like them and they are very convenient and so on.

Does it mean that women are more concerned with the 'look good' syndrome, which is a typical feature of consumer culture? The chapter that follows will specifically look into this question. However, no significant difference is observed in the buying habit of various age groups indicating that the increased buying behaviour is a part of the middle class belonging to all age groups and not something specific to a particular age group.

Loan Trap

Winston has brought in a related aspect that has become integral in the purview of devouring consumerism in the domain of consumer culture:

> There are lots of schemes available today like installments that promote this consumerist tendency. I know some of my neighbours who are average like us, spending a major chunk of the money that they earn for buying expensive and luxurious things. Whenever they are hard of money they invariably borrow loans. And there are moneylenders to make use of this situation – colloquially this system is known as *blade* (debtors are charged with exorbitant interests for the borrowed money as being cut heavily with a sharp blade).

Samir got into the fatal issues involved in this devouring tendency of consumer culture and suggested the direction that shows a way out of the unending trap:

> Now-a-days, people take loans to get vehicles and so on and get into a trap; they seem to avail loans and other similar financial schemes to purchase luxurious commodities and find that they are not able to repay. Some informal lending systems, locally known as *blade,* extract huge interests. An agency conducted a study near my village and found that many were suffering on account of this trap. We discuss at home about the different offers, gifts and other benefits attached to certain items, although we don't go for them. I have noticed that these gifts are mostly attached to cosmetics; but then we prefer those products that are made in our *ayalkoottams* (Neighbourhood Groups) – the *swadhesi* items (indigenous). We want to promote them; they are cost effective, and prepared locally.

Based on his own experience, Franklin explained me the reasons why lower-middle class consumers go about in availing loans:

> When the debt becomes so huge, we repay it by availing *panayam* (taking loans on gold security from financiers). We have to pay around Rs 6,000 per month as interest alone for the amount of money we have borrowed at different occasions. Still we go for all the most modern items, because we should not be lower than our neighbours. Although we have only one income source of about Rs 3,000 per month, by financial adjustments we spend about Rs 5,000. We manage it by rolling money; that is, we get lump sum from others and then, lend it

for interest and other financial adjustments. But I tell you, it's a real botheration ....

These narratives do speak of the ways in which people of the lower-middle class manage different purchasing schemes and benefits. As shown in the Figure 6.3, the quantitative data revealed that some respondents did incur liabilities of loan in their efforts to acquire some of the prestigious items. Ninety-five respondents (26.4% of the total participants) openly acknowledged that they have availed loans in order to get items such as four-wheeler, refrigerator, ornaments, computer, TV, washing machine, clothes, music system, housing, etc.

Figure 6.3

Consumer durables purchased availing loan

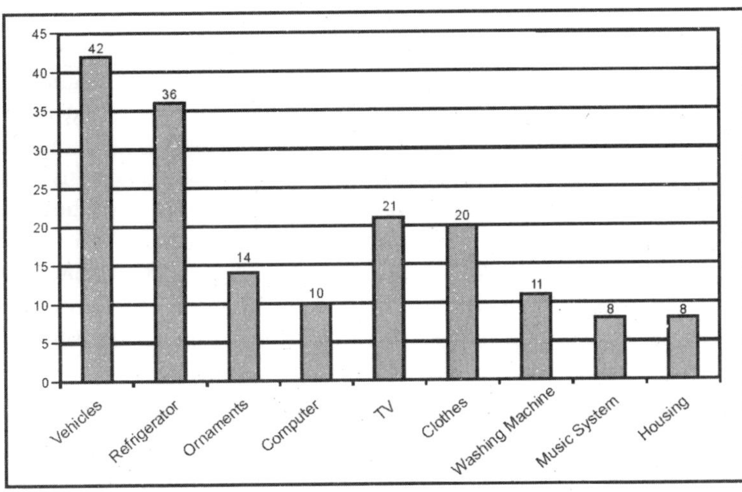

It is revealing that the maximum number of respondents availed loans to purchase four-wheelers. Thus, 42 out of the total number of 95 respondents (44.2%) have taken loans for this purpose. Again, while analyzing the break-up of the data in terms of the income level of those who have availed loans and such schemes, we find that the highest percentage of them (41.1%) hailed from the lower-middle class group. The data, in fact, shows a downward trend in the percentage from the lower-middle to the upper-middle class (Table 6.6). It indicates that it is the lower category of the middle class who undergoes the toughest struggle to show themselves off in this social situation, wherein the market gains ascendancy in shaping the destiny and identity of the people in their everyday lives.

Table 6.6

Income level frequency of the middle class who avail loans and other financial schemes

Income class	*Loans and other financial schemes*		*Total*
	Yes	*No*	
Lower-middle (Rs 5,000–10,000)	39 41.1%	155 58.5%	194 53.9%
Middle-middle (Rs 10,000–15,000)	37 38.9%	80 30.2%	117 32.5%
Upper-middle (Rs 15,000–20,000)	19 20.0%	30 11.3%	49 13.6%
Total	95 100.0%	265 100.0%	360 100.0%

Four-wheelers are considered as a special status symbol among the middle class. It has already been noticed that Franklin, hailing from a lower-middle class setting, cherished highly the day when he would have the honour of possessing a four-wheeler. Quantitative data unambiguously corroborated this fact. Considerable section of the participants (68.1% of the sample) thinks that four-wheelers are bought more as a status symbol than a real need. "Who don't you own a car now? Almost all have it," was the comment Maya made when I talked to her about the issues involved in owning a car today. Santhosh was prepared to speak more on this with a fitting anecdote.

> The middle class people by and large are now crazy about possessing a car; and several of them are availing loan from KSFE (Kerala State Financial Enterprises). But they are not aware of the fact that they are going to be trapped and it would eventually become suicidal. [...] I know the story of my neighbour. He is a middle class man who is working in the Secretariat. He availed himself of the special scheme for car loan from KSFE. At that time his two sons were studying in a

prestigious English Medium School in town. Finally, he had to withdraw them from there and get them into a public school, as he couldn't manage the monthly fees along with the heavy KSFE monthly installment for the car. In the process he lost about Rs 30,000 as interest alone in one year. The end of the story is that he was unable to make the repayment of the loan every month and KSFE confiscated the car.

Maya, who belonged to the upper-middle class, is a typical example that substantiates the case that four-wheelers and their latest models are considered as prestigious status symbol by the middle class. Naturally, the sale of four-wheelers, particularly of the new models, is higher in the state of Kerala.[2] Reghu Dev's plain confession verified this aspect better:

> I have a car. I owned it recently. Car was a fascination for me. I like driving car. It is also related to my status and prestige. My college life is coming to an end. So, now, I can afford a car. [...] I too have my passions. Still I feel that I am an orthodox amidst my friends. Some of them think that if we get into a vehicle, the minimum speed should be sixty. That is a part of showing off oneself and it is also a way of being modern in today's life.

A very high proportion constituting 76 per cent of the respondents considers that the middle class psyche tend to link the latest models of vehicles with social prestige. One fine morning, Maya was overwhelmingly joyful. No wonder she had happy news to report:

> We changed our car. We had a Maruti. Husband wanted to get a Santro and he went for it. Naturally, it is more convenient and comfortable especially with air conditioner, but more than that, it is more glamorous. Most of our relatives have Santro. He had to take a huge sum of loan from Canara Bank to purchase the car. We will not be using it ordinarily. For general purpose we will take the bike.

The age-wise tabulation reveals that the youth and adult categories in higher proportions hold the opinion that four-wheelers and latest models of vehicles are symbols of prestige and status today.

Table 6.7

Age group-wise distribution showing whether four-wheelers are symbols of status and prestige

Age group	*Four-wheelers as status symbol*			*Latest models are prestigious*		
	Yes	*No*	*Total*	*Yes*	*No*	*Total*
15–30	130 *(70.2%) 53.1%	55 (29.8%) 47.8%	185 51.4%	140 (75.7%) 50.9%	45 (24.3%) 52.9%	185 51.4%
31–55	103 (66.5%) 42.0%	52 (33.5%) 45.2%	155 43.1%	120 (77.4%) 43.6%	35 (22.6%) 41.2%	155 43.1%
56–70	12 (60%) 4.9%	8 (40%) 7.0%	20 5.6%	15 (75%) 5.5%	5 (25%) 5.9%	20 5.6%
Total	245 100.0%	115 100.0%	360 100.0%	275 100.0%	85 100.0%	360 100.0%

*Percentages given in parentheses show the frequency within the respective group.

Interestingly, an income-wise break-up of this data shows that the maximum percentage of respondents who consider vehicles as carriers of prestige and status belongs to lower-middle class and middle-middle class sections.

Table 6.8

Income-wise distribution showing if four wheelers and latest models are prestigious status symbols

Income class	*Four-wheelers as status symbol*			*Latest models in vehicles as prestigious*		
	Yes	*No*	*Total*	*Yes*	*No*	*Total*
Lower-middle (Rs 5,000–10,000)	134 (69%) 54.7%	60 (31%) 52.2%	194 53.9%	149 (76.8%) 54.2%	45 (23.2%) 52.9%	194 53.9%
Middle-middle (Rs 10,000–15,000)	83 (70.9%) 33.9%	34 (29.1%) 29.6%	117 32.5%	91 (77.8%) 33.1%	26 (22.2%) 30.6%	117 32.5%
Upper-middle (Rs 15,000–20,000)	28 (57%) 11.4%	21 (43%) 18.3%	49 13.6%	35 (71.4) 12.7%	14 (28.6%) 16.5%	49 13.6%
Total	245 100.0%	115 100.0%	360 100.0%	275 100.0%	85 100.0%	360 100.0%

This again provides us the clue to the reason why many of the middle class people are struggling very hard to acquire a vehicle, preferably a four-wheeler and that too, the latest model. It shows that the advocates and agents of consumer culture have succeeded in instilling the idea that the main ingredients of status and prestige of persons and identities depend upon those commodities, which they project as symbols of status and identity.

Paradox

On the question of appreciating the lifestyle propagated by the advertisements on consumer products, beauty pageants and fashions, the respondents unambiguously proclaimed a stand against it. To this question, 76.4 per cent (275 out of 300) responded negatively. This means that the kind of lifestyle that the new wave of consumer culture emanates is not very acceptable given the mindset of the respondents. This in a way can be taken to be revealing the basic disposition towards the lifestyle that is in tune with the currents of consumer culture in general. On the contrary, among the respondents who expressed the contrary view that they appreciate the lifestyle promoted by the channels of consumer culture, the maximum proportion contributing 64.7 per cent belonged to youth. Moreover, earlier, the data revealed unambiguously that the middle class in general and middle class youth in particular are the most influenced and conditioned by the advertisements and other publicity shows, and so form the primary groups of customers of the consumer culture.

The majority of the respondents were also of the opinion that the lifestyle that advertisements and TV channels promote today does not match with our traditional lifestyle. Seventy per cent of the total sample shared this view, which included 52 per cent of the youth (70.8% of the total participants of youth), 42.9 per cent of the adult (69.7% of the total respondents of the middle group) and 5.2 per cent of the elders (65% of the total respondents from the group of elderly). A very high proportion of the respondents in all these age groups declared that the existing environment that is created by the carriers of consumer culture is incompatible with the traditional life situation of this land prior to the introduction of the kind of lifestyle propounded by consumer culture.

Table 6.9

Age group-wise opinions on whether the lifestyle of the consumer culture matches with our tradition

Age-group	*Appreciating lifestyle of advertisements, fashion shows*		*Advertisements lifestyle does not match with our tradition*		*Total*
	Yes	*No*	*Yes*	*No*	
15–30	55 *(29.8%) 64.7%	130 *(70.2%) 47.3%	131 *(70.8%) 52.0%	54 *(29.2%) 50%	185
31–55	28 *(18.1%) 32.9%	127 *(81.9%) 46.2%	108 *(69.7%) 42.9%	47 *(30.3%) 43.51	155
56–70	2 *(10%) 2.4%	18 *(90%) 6.5%	13 *(65%) 5.2%	7 *(35%) 6.5%	20
Total	85 *(23.6%) 100.0%	275 *(76.4%) 100%	252 *(70%) 100.0%	108 *(30%) 100%	360

*Percentage of the respective age group.

An apparent contradiction is noticed in the perception of the youth as regards the integral ingredients of consumer culture available today. On the one hand, young boys and girls as a whole tend to reject the kind of lifestyle that the advertisements and other similar publicity events strive to promote as part of the spread of consumer culture. On the other hand, they seem to appreciate and become the major beneficiaries and advocates of the same. This contradiction becomes all the more evident when they acknowledge that it is the youth, as a category, is the most influenced by the new rubrics of life and identity dictated by the ambassadors and vehicles of consumer culture.

In the same way, we also find an ambiguous stand in the positions of the middle group (31–35) and the group of elders (56–70). Among the respondents, 46.2 per cent from the middle group and 6.5 per cent from the elderly group pronounced that they did not appreciate the lifestyle advertised by the channels of consumer culture. In fact, these percentages contributed to 81.9 per cent of the adult respondents and 90 per cent of the elders respectively; and we realize that these percentages of the respective groups comprise a very high proportion.

It appears that the position of the respondents belonging to the three age groups, with regard to their acceptability of the lifestyle tied up with consumer culture, points to the idea that the participants in general are oriented against the life-world created by consumer culture. In other words, the majority who participated in the study would like to operate, in principle, from a resistance mode with regard to the trends of globalization. In the light of the inclinations and choices in their practice and behaviour, this ideological stance, is apparently a contradiction. In the final analysis, it appears that there exists a wide gap between the ideal and the real in the perceptions and practices of the middle class people in their response to the manifestations of the all-pervading consumer culture.

At the same time, a sex-wise split up of this data reveals that the percentage of both males and females perceiving likewise remains more or less the same. This once again confirms that there is no substantial difference in the perceptions of the middle class people in terms of sex on the cultural changes brought about on account of the emerging globalization in Kerala.

Table 6.10

Sex-wise opinions on the compatibility of the lifestyle proposed by advertisements, fashion shows etc., with Kerala tradition

Sex	*Appreciating lifestyle of advertisements, fashion shows*	*Advertisements lifestyle does not match with the tradition of Kerala*	*Total*
Male	54 63.5%	155 (69.5%) 61.5%	223
Female	31 36.5%	97 (70.80%) 38.5%	137
Total	85 100.0%	252 100.0%	360

However, when the data regarding the respondents' appreciation or rejection of the lifestyle propagated by the channels of consumer culture is analyzed in terms of the income variable, interestingly the highest proportion of the respondents who appreciate and find it compatible with the tradition of this land, hail from the lower-middle class. About 29 per cent of the lower-middle class (65.9% of the total respondents) appreciated the lifestyle whereas 33 per cent (59.3% of the total respondents) rejected.

In the final analysis, the middle class in general submits to the lifestyle promoted by consumer culture from an accommodative framework and their rhetoric on the compatibility of consumer culture with the indigenous cultural tradition, they seem to operate in a resistance mode. Hence, the behaviour and outlook of the middle class in Kerala towards consumer culture at the micro level exhibit a paradoxical tendency of accommodation and resistance, integration and conflict and negotiation and ambiguity.

Commenting on this aspect of contradiction in the lives of the middle class, social scientists have observed that if the middle class seemed eager to adopt modern lifestyles through the acquisition of consumer goods, they also became the self-appointed protectors of 'tradition' (Nandy, 1990; Van Der Veer, 1994; Mankekar, 1999). This is especially striking in the case of the Hindu middle class, many of whom appeared to have formulated their aspirations in the form of a strident, often exclusionary, nationalism. The people of 1980s generally witnessed the resurgence of religious identities in the political arena. The communalization of nationalism seeped into Doordarshan's construction of 'the Indian past' and its representation of national culture in terms of monolithic and normative Hindu identity.

Middleclassisation

The fact that the lower-middle class is the major group among the middle class who fall within the accommodative framework assumes great significance. The posture of the lower-middle class vis-à-vis consumer culture appears to be somewhat similar to the practice undertaken in a process of 'sanskritization'[3] wherein lower *jatis* try to achieve social mobility and higher status by adopting the religious and social customs of the higher *jatis*. This pervasive tendency of the lower-middle class, who cut across other pertinent categories of sex, age, caste, religion, education, occupation and political party in a globalized context, may be termed as middleclassisation. It denotes the perilous efforts undertaken by a section in India who by virtue of their income and assets fall just above those identified as poor, and may be termed as lower-middle class, in order to rise to the levels of status and prestige hitherto monopolized by the middle class sections well above them.

The crucial feature of the post-capitalistic era seems to be that the lower rungs of middle class, irrespective of religious, caste, creed and political affiliations, as insistent agents and advocates of consumer culture, are trying to seek social mobility and status elevation. Hence, it is likely that the contestations and negotiations of social mobility and status occur at the intersection of diverse income groups from within the middle class in the ambience of consumer culture. So, the domain of consumer culture carves out the sociological boundaries of the middle class, transcending all other boundary-constructing categories, such as religion, community, region and politics. This is how the middle class, which is otherwise regarded as a heterogeneous historical bloc with differing access to relations of production, status and political power, is brought under a homogeneous umbrella. In this sense, the middle class is not a pure economic construct; rather it constitutes a cultural reality tending to generate middle class materiality as well as mentality, imbibing like-mindedness in certain values, tastes, ideology and demands.

The struggles of the lower-middle class in contesting and negotiating the practices and styles of consumption spearheaded by the prevailing ambit of consumer culture could be explained by applying embourgeoisement thesis.[4] This refers to the process by which bourgeois aspirations become institutionalized among the working class. The embourgeoisement debate[5] on British class structure rests on the idea that the working class is increasingly adopting middle class mores and attitudes to the extent that the differences among various social class are becoming less significant, as members of all classes come to share similar patterns of consumption and social behaviour. The term conceptualizes the ways of living evident in the practices of conspicuous consumption with its related capitalistic value system, which are characteristics of the advanced capitalist societies.

In the present-day Indian context of ever increasing absorption of consumer culture by the lower-middle class in the wake of globalization, the embourgeoisement thesis would mean the creation of a mass market for the middle class consumers and the elevation of the aspirations of the lower income middle class to the living standards and lifestyles of the groups that are above them in terms of income, and capitalistic in terms of the values and priorities in life. The natural outcome of this phenomenon will be the integration of the rank, and file workers and lower income labourers who are supposed to be falling into the camp of the working class according to the conventional Marxian dictum in order to form the massive section of the proletariat to lead the class struggle against the capitalist class, with those middle range classes just above them. The capitalist bloc will get subsequently weakened as this lower-middle class joins the mainstream middle class bloc accumulating more and more typical middle class value systems of individualism, security consciousness and extravagance to the tune of exhibiting status and prestige. To put it in simple terms, it may be described as the consumption that constitutes middle class bourgeois mentality in the age of globalization.

As a result, a large majority of the people constitutes a homogeneous bloc in terms of consumer practices and behaviour and are being knit together by assimilating an individualistic outlook and identification with the objectives of the post-capitalist enterprises. They subsequently discard the traditional loyalties of workmates, trade union and class. Instead, the apparent growth of a typically middle class concern with status and social image makes them more family-minded and home-centred and lesser and lesser socially sensitive and collectively conscious. Not so long ago, the middle class was easily identifiable by dress, habits and opinions, shared values and aspirations. They are the people caught between the thin crust of the aristocracy above, and the mass of workers below.

Therefore, the middle class as a category characterized by their consumer habit could be described as a section of the population with vast differences within itself in values, aspirations, earning capacity, taste and style; but they have enough money to enjoy a certain amount of freedom. They form the consuming class according to the market terminology. Capitalistic values come to dominate their world-view that is oriented to seeking personal gains, security, status, prestige and respectability by individualistic rather than collective means, which in other words may be termed as typically middle class values. In this sense, middle classeness is to be regarded as a structure of mentality or the habitation of a safe space that distinguishes one from the less fortunate others.

Notes

1. For an elaborate exposition on this phenomenon, see Dipankar Gupta (2000), *Mistaken Identity: India Between Worlds,* New Delhi: Harper Collins Publishers, pp. 1–99.
2. For instance, Sachio Yamazachi, the Managing Director of Toyota Kirloskar Motors has stated that for Toyota Qualis, Kerala is the best market in India (*Malayala Manorama,* October 14, 2002, p. 5).
3. It refers to the efforts of certain *jatis* to seek promotion within the caste hierarchy by adopting the practices of higher *varnas,* which can result in promotion within their *varna* but not between *varna.* M. N. Srinivas first used it in the context of Indian caste system in his study on *Religion and Society among Coorgs of South India* (1952). Later, some sociologists attempted to extend the term beyond the Indian situation, and to apply it to the analysis of the South African system of apartheid, and even to the system of racial segregation in some parts of the United States during the twentieth century. See Lloyd Warner 'An American Dilemma' in *American Journal of Sociology* (1936) and 'Gunnar Myrdal' in *An American Dilemma* (1944).
4. The concept has Marxian origins. In the late 1880s, Engels attempted to explain the failure of the British working class to exploit the franchise of 1867 in terms of the workers' craving for respectability, and enjoyment of a standard of living sufficient to encourage bourgeois values, lifestyles and political ideals. In its most general

formulation, the concept claimed that the sectoral transformation in the structure of labouring in the new knowledge-based occupations created high levels of class mobility and led to a shrinkage of the working class, considered as a proportion of working class literally becoming more middle class, in the demographic sense at least.

5. The thesis prompted a number of important sociological debates in the 1960s. In the 1980s, commentators of both the extreme Right and Left argued that working class support for the policies of right-wing governments across Europe and North America provided testimony to a new consensus around middle class norms, values and lifestyle (Marshal Gordon, 1994, *Oxford Dictionary of Sociology,* UK: Oxford University Press).

CHAPTER 7

Parameters of Identity

Invested with meaning, commodities 'speak' to consumers. The symbolic meanings of commodities and consumption have been analyzed by scholars such as Arjun Appadurai (1996a) and Dick Hebdige (1979), who focus on the 'social life of things' and on the communicative aspects of consumption, respectively. Since it is embedded in larger significatory chains, consumption necessarily involves the production of meanings. In a consumer cultural environment, the middle class becomes easily identifiable not by their income level, rather by the desires, buying habits and possessions of goods and services, or in other words, status and values. That means what they tend to buy and possess would render their status and prestige which ultimately constitute their identity. Winston's perception directly points to this vital dimension in the making of the contemporary middle class identity in Kerala:

> Certain items have become status symbols in our society today. For instance, we bought a washing machine recently, not because we really needed it, but because it was a status symbol. Some two years back shoes were a compulsory thing for me, thinking that to be glamorous and stylish shoes are essential. But now I don't feel like that since I am aware of the danger involved in such thinking.

Franklin was more forthright in disclosing the question of status and prestige with which the middle class attach to consumer durables:

> In our house, we borrow money and get all the items we want. Mother is more interested than me in acquiring luxurious goods; because she feels that when neighbours have certain items, which we don't have, we are below them. Hence, we got furniture, round table and other appliances on loan. We are also planning to change our flooring, and renovate it with latest marble chips. Certain items we got through installment scheme; items like bed, mattress, fans, etc. All the conveniences are available to us these days. We have to avail all that. Now, I got my two-wheeler on loan. We also plan to buy a car by taking loan. These days we get special loan for car. Without these, we cannot enjoy life now. Everybody enjoys it. Then why should not we?

As Franklin states, "We should not be lower than our neighbours" seems to the cherished slogan that governs the life of middle class in general, especially those who belong to lower-middle class. Hence, if consumption represents the psychological competition for status, then middle class society is the institutionalization of envy. We now move on to see the specific aspects of identity construction of the middle class in Kerala, with special reference to gender and youth as categories requiring separate treatment.

'Look Good' Syndrome

Since the explosion of the mass media in the early 1990s, fashion has brought into living rooms in glossy spreads, fresh from the nation's nascent fashion industry. The arrival of MNCs has had an impact. Their emphasis on design appeal, coupled with the post-liberalization plethora of choices, led to a marketing boom. The new moneyed middle class want to flaunt their wealth; designer tags seem to be the easiest route. As the social changes warranted more parties, outings and gatherings, the emphasis on being attired for the occasion began to take root. "The trickle of fashion followers has become a torrent," observes K. Sunil

Thomas in an article titled "Passion for Fashion – Middle Class Swept by Winds of Change". Title, although typically journalistic in style, aptly captures the mood of the fashion world in recent times:

> The youth spend more money on clothes and accessories than on food. Everyone is following fashion now. ... People are judged by their appearance. The prime considerations for choosing clothes and accessories how good they look (75). Today trends proliferate not just in 'fashion cities', but from the backwater cruise discotheque of Kochi to the ... (*The Week*, May 19, 2002, pp. 74–78).

Seema, a postgraduate student, captured my attention among her other companions for her simplicity in appearance and style. During one of my conversations with her, she told me, "I don't wear *pottu*."[1] This naturally made me inquisitive because I have been under the impression that wearing a *bindi* on the forehead of a young Malayali girl of her age is quite natural as a custom. Later, she explained:

> I am trained like that. I don't like much make up. I have my values and interests. My personality lies not in dressing too much, not on these externals. I know that some give undue importance to these peripherals. But then they get stuck in them.

Later I had occasions to listen to her more about the state of the art with regard to dress, beauty and appearance:

> I am not interested in buying too much, or going after fashions and so on. Till recently, my father used to get clothes for me. I know that my friends in general buy things in plenty today, especially fashionable clothes, cosmetics, etc. They want to be more fashionable and to be modern, to get acceptance among peers. The belief seems to be that people bestow more acceptances and attach more prestige if things are more costly and attractive. I come from a rural background about twenty kilometers away from Quilon town. Even there, I find students becoming very modern in dress, with very expensive sandals, costumes, and so on.

Quantitative response clearly revealed the fact that there are notable changes in the dressing style of young girls in Kerala compared to ten years ago. A very high proportion of respondents who contribute 76.9 per cent of the total sample do agree that the dressing style and the concept of fashion have undergone mammoth changes in recent years. It is observed that the presumed membership in an income class and changes in the fashion world are the major elements which influence middle class people's style of dressing (Figure 7.1).

Figure 7.1

Variables influencing the dressing style of the middle class

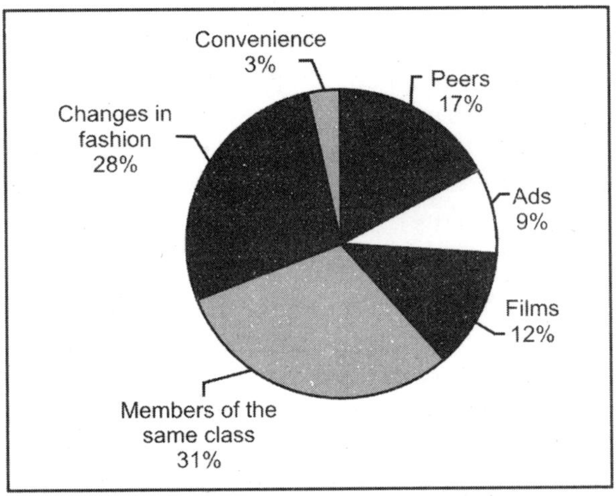

Thus, we have 41.7 per cent of respondents who consider that the members of the same class and occupation mainly influence their style of dressing, and a slightly lesser percentage that constitutes 37.5 per cent views that they are under the influence of the world of fashion with regard to their dressing style. Higher percentage of participants (51.9%) are prompted to change their style of dressing mainly when they found that better brands have come in the market and further (36.7%) when they noticed that new fashions are available in the market.

More significantly, the highest percentage of respondents making this perception comprise the youth themselves (Table 7.1). It is one's belief that motivates one into action. There exists a close association between the belief of the youth with regard to the role of fashionable and latest models of dress in shaping one's image and their practice which apparently results in noticeable changes in their dressing style.

Table 7.1

Sex-wise and age group-wise break-up of the perception of the changes in young girls' dressing pattern

Sex	*Age group*	*Notable changes in young girls' dressing*		*Total*
		Yes	*No*	
Male	15–30	79 49.4%	27 42.9%	106 47.5%
	31–55	69 43.1%	31 49.2%	100 44.8%
	56–70	12 7.5%	5 7.9%	17 7.6%
	Total	160 100.0%	63 100.0%	223 100.0%
Female	15–30	69 59.0%	10 50.0%	79 57.7%
	31–55	46 39.3%	9 45.0%	55 40.1%
	56–70	2 1.7%	1 5.0%	3 2.2%
	Total	117 100.0%	20 100.0%	137 100.0%

However, no significant difference is noticed in the variables like sex and education in the above case. It highlights the fact that in the age of globalization, factors such as fashion, brands and class positions (income class) do play important roles in defining the parameters of identity, irrespective of the categories such as sex, education and religion. It is not surprising when a very high proportion of respondents who constituted 76.9 per cent of the total sample perceive that there are notable changes in the dressing style of young girls in Kerala from that of ten years ago.

It is interesting to note that more than half of the respondents believe that fashionable clothes improve the self-image of women. It points to the fact that there is a sizeable section in the middle class who considers that the latest fashion and newer brands of dress do contribute in the make up of one's personality and appearance. As we saw in the previous chapters, this belief is generated by the manner in which ideas on beauty, appearance and self-worth are injected by the commercial advertisement on clothes in various media.

Table 7.2

Sex-wise and age group-wise tabulation of the opinions on whether fashionable clothes improve women's image

Sex	*Age group*	*Fashionable clothes improve women's image*		*Total*
		Yes	*No*	
Male	15–30	62 54.9%	44 40.0%	106 47.5%
	31–55	45 39.8%	55 50.0%	100 44.8%
	56–70	6 5.3%	11 10.0%	17 7.6%
	Total	113 100.0%	110 100.0%	223 100.0%
Female	15–30	44 60.3%	35 54.7%	79 57.7%
	31–55	28 38.4%	27 42.2%	55 40.1%
	56–70	1 1.4%	2 3.1%	3 2.2%
	Total	73 100.0%	64 100.0%	137 100.0%

Notwithstanding, a break-up of this data on the basis of sex and age group variables bring out some further details on this. In all the age groups, the percentage of the youth is higher among those who opine that fashionable clothes improve women's image; among the youth, young girls predominantly share this view (Table 7.2). It is the middle class young girls who are more preoccupied with the change of fashion and trends vis-à-vis image consciousness. Corroborating on this data, Samir had the following observation:

> I studied in Arts College in BA Economics department. It had all the characteristics of a city culture. I have mingled with all kinds of students there. Most of my friends were from middle-income group. The way they talk, the pattern of their dress, even their friendship, I found very mechanical. They used to change their attire and outlook every week or month, or according to the dresses that heroines and heroes of the movies and other models in the ads wear.

Beauty Lust

It is very evident that middle class youth as a category is the most influenced by the present-day cult of look and appearance propagated by the advocates and agents of consumer culture as part of the spread of globalization. Adding to this, Seema spoke to me on the dimensions that lead to the entire world of the changed concept of look, appearance and beauty:

> Appearance has become very important today. Look is a serious concern. People need attention and they need to be looked at. They feel happy about that. A new concept of beauty is propagated in the media, advertisements etc. The physical measurements of girls and what should constitute their physical structure are all instructed in the media events and spectacles. And many follow them, because they think that it is the ideal of beauty. Certain companies have their vested agenda to sell their products. But I do not want get into their trap.

Annie with the sentiments of a mother shared with me the 'beauty preoccupations' of her children that in fact add to her 'motherly worries':

> My children tell me that we as parents need to be beautiful and should have good appearance. Even my little girl who is seven years old is very much conscious of beauty. She wants to use lipstick. [...] Girls want to imitate heroines in the movies because they consider them as their models. Now-a-days there are fashion show competitions for the beauty queens and the best model. It is only to promote cosmetics and the cosmetic industry is flourishing day by day.
>
> What worries me now is that they make it a point to go to beauty parlour even for a hair cut. They want to visit these

> centres especially when we have to go for some special functions. My son enjoys going there and getting face wash etc. In my younger days there were no such things. *'Look'* has become very very important today.

Bobby admitted that he definitely spends more money on cosmetics than ten years ago. He thinks, "Beauty consciousness has increased and 'appearance syndrome' is undoubtedly on the high. Correspondingly, the use of cosmetics too has increased. Everywhere we find advertisements on cosmetics. Prakash makes a penetrating introspection as he commented on this:

> I am conscious of my *Look* to a certain extent. I know that varieties of cosmetics and their ads in the media do influence me in shaping my notions of beauty and appearance, because they generate newer aspirations. For instance, there is the ad of Sachin Tendulkar appearing as the brand ambassador for TVS Victor and making an impact on the sale of it. We feel like possessing things that he advocates. In general, the *look* has become very important, even to the extent of the sole criterion for getting the attraction of the opposite sex.

In the quantitative response, a very high percentage of respondents is of the opinion that people of Kerala in general purchase more cosmetic items compared to ten years ago (Figure 7.2).

Figure 7.2

Perception regarding the increase of the purchase of cosmetics

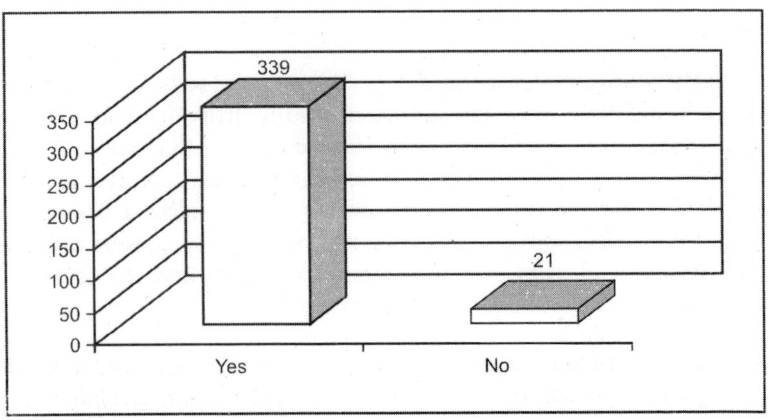

Hence, we have 339 participants consisting of 94.2 per cent of the sample, as against the remaining negligible portion of 5.8 per cent who consider that cosmetics are the major items whose consumption has increased substantially since the onset of consumer culture. Franklin unambiguously remarked about this heightened sense 'look good syndrome' that is observed in both boys and girls vis-à-vis the increased cosmetic business:

> Look is very important now both for gents and ladies. They want to dress up maximum. Especially girls believe that cosmetics improve their personality and confidence. Now, cosmetic business has gone so high. To sell cosmetics they conduct shows and competitions and also select people from the third world in order to increase demand for their products. Girls from village think that by using cosmetics their value increases and so they buy these products. Modelling too begets lot of demand. My sister is very much interested in these. Every day she removes her nail polish, and use colours suitable to her dress and so on.

Seema added her case, complementing Franklin's comment:

> My aunty is a beautician and she has lots of customers and her beauty parlour is located in the close vicinity of a college. It is a good business for her. Mostly, I find ordinary people coming to her beauty parlour. Students, teachers, housewives all come there. She conducted a fashion show recently and I too joined. It was held in Pathanamthitta near her centre. The show was part of the function of a women's group and my aunty has taken the initiative to organize it because she wanted to attract more customers to her centre.

These testimonies ascertain that the middle class sections in Kerala seem to have succumbed to the 'business of beauty' along with its portend 'look good syndrome' that is a characteristic feature of consumer culture.

Looking at the quantitative data in terms of age and sex variables, it is found that the highest percentage of respondents hail from the age group of 15–30, constituting 52.8 per cent of the total sample, who regard that the purchase of cosmetics has definitely taken a big hike since the last decade. This proportion of youth as a single category making more than half of the total respondents, who share this view, is really significant. If we break up the youth category further, we note that more particularly, it is the young girls who predominate compared to their male counterparts. Thus, young girls, comprising 57.9 per cent of the respondents, believe that there is definitely an increase in the buying of various cosmetic articles. This proportion of young middle class girls constitutes 97.5 per cent of the total women participants in the study; and 56.2 per cent that is well above the half of the total number of female participants in the study, leaving only the negligible portion of 2.5 per cent females who shared the contrary view.

Table 7.3

Opinion on the increase of the purchase of cosmetics according to sex and age group

Sex	*Age group*	*Purchase more cosmetics*		Total
		Yes	*No*	
Male	15–30	102 *(96.2%) 49.5%	4 *(3.8%) 23.5%	106 47.5%
	31–55	87 42.2%	13 76.5%	100 44.8%
	56–70	17 8.3%	0	17 7.6%
	Total	206 100.0%	17 100.0%	223 100.0%
Female	15–30	77 *(97.5%) 57.9%	2* (2.5%) 50.0%	79 57.7%
	31–55	54 40.6%	1 25.0%	55 40.1%
	56–70	2 1.5%	1 25.0%	3 2.2%
	Total	133 100.0%	4 100.0%	137 100.0%

*Percentage in terms of the respective age group vis-à-vis sex.

Therefore, the predominant category that forms the major consumers of the 'look good syndrome' in the backdrop of the all-pervasive consumer culture has to be identified as young middle class girls. By citing a reference to her niece's 'beauty craze,' Maya narrated her experience of visiting beauty parlours:

> My niece who is a graduate student goes to beauty parlours very frequently. For her, it is part of her timetable that periodically she makes it a point to go to beauty parlour. By the way, I too have visited beauty parlours, but not as frequently as my niece; may be for some special functions. But I tell you it is a nice experience to go there. We feel good and feel like a different person once we come out of it. The cost depends on what are the items we want to do there. I normally do facial, bleaching and eyebrow shaping and this would cost a maximum of Rs 200.

This also points to the fact that it is this group of young middle class girls that appears to be the most accommodative of the consumer market. "Feeling good is looking good" seems to be an important slogan that influences young girls in the ambience of consumer culture.

Along with girls, gents too seem to be so much preoccupied with this business of 'look' and 'beauty.' Here is an indicative remark on this new trend. Sejal Shah, in a characteristically journalistic style, observes:

> That beauty salons, once the exclusive preserve of women, are bursting with men, their faces well 'masked' and feet and hands stretched out for the beautician's attention. Hair on the head is styled to suit the face and that on the chest and legs is ripped off with hot wax. Appearances do matter in these dog-eat-dog days of global competition [...] Men are becoming conscious about their looks (*The Week*, March 30, 1997, p. 34).

The article further says that in India, the concept of the well-groomed male came in with liberalization. "All of a sudden even the common people became aware of designer brands like Reebok, Armani, Rolex and Piaget and the awareness came through television and other media" (p. 36). It attributes to the arrival of foreign companies and the media exposure to the global outlook. Another reason for this consciousness is the manifold increase in the Indian consumer market for men. In this context, Prakash observed that men rather than women visited beauty parlours more:

> We can find any number of gent's beauty parlours and massaging centres in every nook and corner. Even my village, which is typically a rural area, has got beauty parlours. Although I don't go myself, I know personally that there are some very ordinary, middle class customers who regularly go for massaging and facial; some of them are my own friends. One is a vehicle broker, about twenty-five years old. It comes to Rs 300 to Rs 350 each time.

Young men seem to believe that confidence comes with good grooming, which is very important for their job and social standing. With more and more middle class males putting their best foot forward to look good, the cosmetic industry thrives, so much so that male cosmetics are the fastest growing market internationally.[2] With the policies of globalization and liberalization, there has been an unprecedented growth in the beauty industry. One day I had a chance to talk to Santhosh about this burgeoning business:

> Gent's beauty parlours shoot up like anything; now there are even mobile parlours [...] I too went for a facial in connection with a marriage function. I spent about Rs 375. I feel that it is okay going to a beauty parlour when there are special functions. We feel good and confident with flashy cheeks and so on. ...

The market has grown because men have realized that it is high time they looked and smelt good. The foreign companies have seen the potential among the middle classes and are brainwashing them. "Cosmetics maketh the man," seems to be the new dictum. And so the average Malayali as a middle class person seems to believe that beauty care is the key to feel nice, to look good and to climb the social ladder.

Cult of the Body

Nevertheless, Maya considers this new interest in the business of beauty as a universal phenomenon spread among all categories and sections in the society:

> Not only the youth who is influenced by these new trends, but all categories of people irrespective of age, sex, religion and politics. Some are frustrated that they are not able to afford it because of the financial constraints although they aspire very much to move according to these new trends. It is true that Women's magazines and so on generate more appetite for this by providing the required seductive info and tips.

In a cover story article of *India Today*, Anupama Chopra and Farah Baria while talking about this soaring "beauty business", begins with the great satellite invasion. "Television is constantly beaming these beautiful people into our living rooms", and "the quest for beauty has become guilt free and aspirational in an entrepreneurial society on the move". According to them, today an average working woman spends nearly a third of her salary on beautifying herself (November 15, 1996, pp. 45–55).

It will be revealing to examine some of the following plausible reasons for the soaring increase in the purchase of more cosmetic items compared to ten years ago (Figure 7.3):

Figure 7.3

Reasons for the increase in the purchase of cosmetics

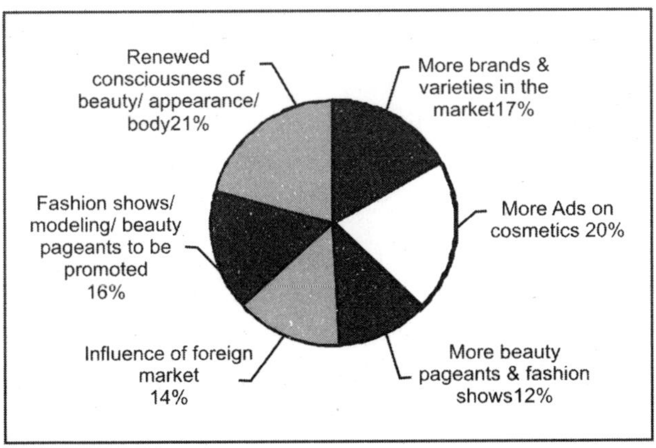

(1) Availability of more brands and varieties of cosmetics in the market since the last decade (36.9%).
(2) More advertisements on cosmetics (44.7%).
(3) Higher number of spectacles such as beauty pageants, fashion shows etc. (26.3%).
(4) Highly liberalized entry of foreign market and its influence (31.1%).
(5) Generation of a renewed consciousness of beauty, appearance and body (45.6%).

As Prem Kumar has put it bluntly: "Now everybody has a craze for beauty [...] wants glamour. So we have lots of beauty parlours and the middle class people rush to these centres heavily."

In fact, all these reasons are interrelated and are dependent on each other. Moreover, they are all related to the phenomenon of globalization and its marked consumer culture. Therefore, all these proposed reasons are to be taken together as pointing to the definitive changes that the advent of globalization has brought in the lifestyle and value system of the middle class people. It has to be specially noted that with regard to the reasons for the increase in the purchase of cosmetics, the highest percentage of participants consider that there are a development of a new concept of beauty, appearance and body. According to Anil, there are a number of interrelated phenomena connected to the business of beauty, look and cosmetics. He says:

> [...] even in Thiruvananthapuram we have frequent programmes of fashion shows, beauty pageants and modelling. Those companies who sponsor these shows really exploit people. The clients who watch this tend to imitate as it creates the feeling that those who are involved in this are great and worthy of imitation.

An explosion of the beauty industry has given rise to widespread proliferation of favourable attitudes towards the 'glamour' industries such as modelling. In this connection, Santhosh recollected his experience of taking part in a fashion show which he relates to this culture of the business of beauty which has crept in recently in the lives of the middle class:

> Beauty consciousness has definitely increased. You know why? The models that appear in ads are invariably beautiful. Seeing them everybody wants to be beautiful [...] Modelling too is like that. I too had the fortune to be a model in a function at my college. I felt great; as though I got elevated to a celestial state. At that time people like film star Madhavan and so on were present for the programme. Feeling so great *yaar*. ...

During a conversation on the 'cosmetic industry' and 'the business of beauty' Maya made a poignant comment:

> [...] the reason for such a widespread interest in cosmetics is because there are lots of ads on fashion and modelling, etc. Lots of students have gone into such fields to become models and anchors which brought them big glamour and fame. So, students must be thinking that if they also move according to the current trend, they also become great and glamorous. But I don't like myself or others whom I like, going into that field. It may affect our family bonding and we will also be forced to exhibit us.

Maya's remark that "[...] I don't like myself or others whom I like going into that field. It may affect our family bonding and we will also be forced to exhibit us," is a pertinent point that requires further reflection. In the backdrop of the flourishing 'cosmetic industry' that thrives on the created 'look good syndrome' in the domain of consumer culture, there is an argument that the emphasis on physical appearance means to be preoccupied with sensuality and externals; for instance, how the skin feels and smells, the colour, sheen and cut of hair. Prem Kumar touched upon this aspect of 'look good syndrome' that consumer culture consciously cultivates with the thriving cosmetic industry. He declares:

> I watch F channel. But I don't want my kith and kin to go for modelling and fashion shows. I know that people will look at us with contempt. Modelling and Fashion shows have now turned out to be NOT an exhibition of new dresses and patterns, but they have actually become shows without any dress. F channel type of things and shows has already come in Kerala. Many in our society are going for modelling. I know

> some of my friends who are into modelling. Modelling means fashion shows. But you know that they are going astray and are exploited. Even if they do not want they will later be forced to. But in between they amass lot of money and have a jolly good life. Business people want to promote these nasty ideas on body and sex.

The point that Prem Kumar is trying to make here is that cosmetic marketing sets a new standard in people's relationship with their bodies. Men and women are now obliged to maintain a certain image, as an attribute of their masculinity and femininity. The efforts involved in cultivating the appearance today necessitate the continuous acquisition of a growing number of commodities. In the changed culture of the market, "happiness amounts to beauty and being sexy". In this process of gaining a new face and body, one simultaneously confronts the fate of losing one's own. This way consumer culture is likely to build on fears and unsatisfied longings, defining the body in a new fashion, both its look and its smell, as well as its tactile sense and self-perception. In this sense, a new cult of the body seems to have taken its roots in society wherein the middle class young men and women seem to have risen as the ardent 'beauty ritual performers and devotees'. Beauty parlours are likely to be the 'temples' par excellence initiating the potential devotees and performing the 'cult of the body'. In the final analysis, these are some of the ways in which commodity aesthetics take possession of the middle class. Quantitative query on this question substantiated these perceptions and remarks.

Sexualization Project

From the perspective of the political economy, sponsor companies are looking to less developed countries in Asia and Africa and to countries of the former socialist bloc which have opened up their economies to sell a form of demeaning market-driven entertainment that has become unacceptable elsewhere. In other words, in the globalized world-view, beauty is not so much in the eye of the beholder as in the cash registers of related companies. There are clear links between globalization and the accelerated commoditization of women. Brinda Karat, ideologue of the left wing Women's Association, submits that "the growing obsession with 'looking good' is not a reflection of the growing confidence of the independent-minded 'modern miss,' as is often suggested by the mainstream media." On the contrary, this constitutes oppressive pressure on young middle class women and distorts their self-worth (*Frontline,* December 13, 1996, p. 14).

The quantitative response to the contemporary cultural processes and the perceived changes in relation to the current form of globalization further illuminates us on this debate. A majority of the participants comprising 76.9 per cent of the total sample are unambiguous in their position that they do not appreciate the kind of image and view of woman depicted in commercial advertisements, beauty pageants and fashion shows. Again, an absolute majority of participants, constituting 73.9 per cent, therefore, think that those spectacles dealing with the concept, exhibition and promotion of beauty, appearance and body come in conflict with the culture and tradition of this land. This is a general perception that is shared by all categories of the respondents, irrespective of the variables such as age, sex, religion and income.

In the cultural environment of globalization wherein the ideal of commodity aesthetics becomes delivering the absolute minimum use of value, disguised and staged by a maximum of seductive illusion, all objects of use assume a sexual form to a great extent. This project of *sexualization* of life seems to be built into the very fabric of consumer culture. Sarup (1996) has maintained that with the help of fashion, people are advertising all of the above-mentioned objects as sexual beings. Higher proportion of the participants, comprising 59.4 per cent, thinks that the sexual overtones in the commercial advertisements and other such spectacles undertaken by the market magnates for the sale of consumer products influence their concept of body.

Maya feels beyond doubt that the image of body, especially that of the female, has been degraded. Woman's body is treated as a commodity and so body exhibition and exposure is considered as desirable. In the process, women themselves are regarded as 'commodities'. This is the objectification detour that is being manoeuvred in the cultural arena of globalization wherein we find a general sexualization of commodities, especially that of human beings. The new equation that the consumer culture demonstrates is that *being young equals being sexually attractive*. Consequently, there is the threat of sexual ageing and isolation, which results in a universal compulsion for people to 'cosmetize' themselves and also the interior of their homes. In short, the concept of beauty and body images proves that the cosmetic industry along with the fashion and beauty spectacles has exercised a strong impact on shaping gender images.

It may be well argued at this point that the site of the body is that site which is dissociated from its subject, amounts to an icon that is re-sacralized to signify the manifestation of order. Reverting to Durkheimian notion of god, which necessitates a certain notion of society, here emerges as a certain notion of society from a certain notion of body. Now, the cultural representation of the body is linked to the making of contemporary middle class ethos. Correspondingly, the site of identity shifts from the more conspicuous categories such as nation, blood and language to the view of the body.

One day I was fortunate to get Prakash, Annie and Maya around a table to engage in a discussion on the issue of commodification of women and sexualization of life in the present-day social environment of consumer culture. In the midst of the heated discussion, Prakash argued that the unprecedented increase in the rate of prostitution, trafficking, dowry deaths, divorces and other such atrocities against women that has become the order of contemporary Keralite society, will have to be located on the project of sexualization of humans, which is inextricably linked to the currents of consumer culture. In a response to Prakash, Annie's distressing comment as a concerned mother was to the point:

> Everywhere we have fashion shows, beauty pageants, etc. These are all new trends as far as our society is concerned. The problem is that correspondingly drastic changes have crept in the attitude towards girls. As a result, social environment has become very very fearful. I will not allow my girl-child to be alone at home. [...] I am literally afraid. [...] We can't believe anybody now.

Responding to these sentiments, Maya made her stand on the matter which is clear:

> Now in the name of personality development, lots of vulgarity is there. It affects our culture and tradition ... boy girl relationship ... our attitude to elders ... Importance is attached to externals. It is imitation of the west [...] these are recent trends; during my college days we did not have these tendencies. But I cannot accept many aspects in it.

This poignant discussion was quite insightful. It reminds anyone about the predominant tendency inherent in the middle class to be accommodative to the vicissitudes of globalization on the one hand, and at the same time manifest moral ambiguities, negotiations and contradictory positions on the other hand, which has already been brought to surface in the previous chapters. At another level, it opens up vistas of the debate on cultural flows related to the project of globalization as it dwells on the cultural ramifications of the global market and its dynamics as it is being played out in the everyday destiny of the middle class.

Culture is a form of highly participatory activity, in which people construct their identities and organize their way of life. It has been found that it is a consumer culture in the wider purview of globalization that provides the material and resources to constitute identities in contemporary society, especially to the middle class. In this new mode of identity-kit, the look, style, and image become the predominant constituents. One of the defining features of this contemporary culture seems to be the fragmentation, transitoriness, and multiplicity of identities and subsequent forms of subjectivities. This, in a way, has marked a radical shift from the earlier mode of cultural milieu wherein constituents such as moral, political, and existential choices and commitments mostly constituted individual identity. Now-a-days, the look, the style and the image seem to constitute the parameters of identity. Subsequently, the cultural scenario of Kerala too is charged with the renewed interest in the affairs and issues of 'showing off' and 'exhibiting' looks and beauty. This, in a way, points to the direction in which cultural transformations occur in a given region when it is brought under the influence of consumer culture.

Digitalized Status

The new global territories are increasingly becoming the venues for social, political, economic and cultural creolization. The use of new communicational technologies in international financial transactions has given rise to a hyper-space of 'fast capitalism,' as the global flow of capital, energy, goods and people speeds up to accompany the proliferation of images, simulations and symbols. Hence, globalization is being accompanied by the emergence of a 'cyberspace,' more specifically a 'telesphere,' which is coextensive with, but distinct from, the natural biosphere and the industrial technosphere. It is composed of "... artificial spaces created by streams of data, audio and video. In this third nature, there are innumerable new regions of action, developing their own agendas, interests and values beyond, behind and beneath the nation state" (Massey, 1994, p. 93).

Today, we witness a blossoming form of communicational and informational technologies linking computer, television, satellite, cable and mobile phone. Space has been 'technologically eliminated'. The instantaneity of 'real time' coverage on global television means that we can be both in 'there' and 'here'. Harvey's (1989) account of the history of time-space compression advances the case that market forces have always been at its heart. What we understand as the 'here and now' of territory is being redefined globally by the new technologies linking satellites and televisions, telephones and computers. The 'real-time' of telecommunications – 'action-at-distance' – has superseded the 'real space' of immediate action. The whole world is available to the gaze of orbiting satellites, so much so that we can now talk of a 'tele-present,' or 'a real time, tele-reality is supplanting the reality of the real-space presence of objects and places. It is the media practices that really rearranged our senses of space and time.

At another occasion, Maya appeared to be more practical and realistic. This time she was talking about the story of the purchase of a computer at home. She says:

> We have a computer at home. It was not a real need for us, and so it has almost become like a decoration. In the initial days after purchase, my husband used to spend some time before it writing some letters and so on. But now he doesn't bother even

> that much. We just got it, that's all. Since most of the officers at husband's firm decided to get a computer, he also wanted one. He likes to get items like that. He takes more interest in getting such expensive and costly home appliances like microwave oven. I may sometimes think why we should go for those items, as they are very costly and are not very necessary. But he just likes to purchase and keep them in positions. He enjoys that.

However, quantitative response to the use of Internet and cyber technology revealed something different. Among the various uses of the Internet that the respondents enlisted, 'access to latest information' appears to be the most prominent. Among the total of 227 respondents, 63.1 per cent said that Internet provides access to the latest information across the world. Along with this, as mentioned by 82 respondents (22.8% of the total sample), Internet enables one to keep abreast of the latest in every field. This is followed by another important utility perceived by 55.1 per cent of respondents that Internet provides the possibility of fast and cheap communication, far and near. A small percentage of 20.8 (75 respondents) believed that Internet would give scope for lots of fun and pleasure. Still an insignificant portion of the respondents (3.6% of the total sample) considered that Internet would enhance status and self-image (Figure 7.4).

Figure 7.4

Different uses of Internet according to respondents

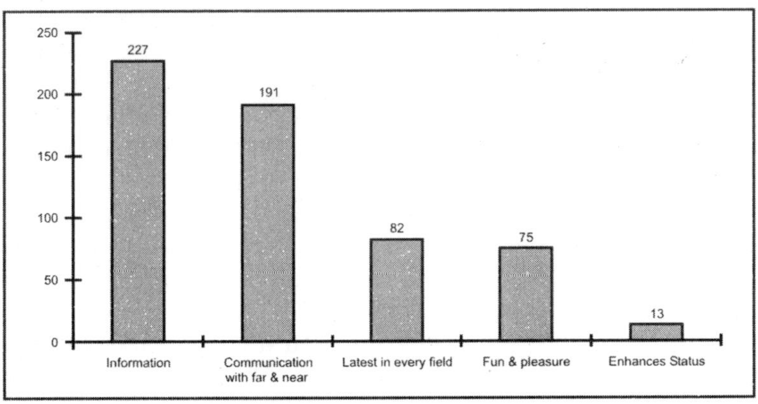

Nevertheless, we need to explore further the meaning of the statement that "Internet gives scope for lots of fun". It is indicative of the cultural rupture brought about by the advent of the latest technology, making cyber highways for the growth and spread of globalization across the world. For instance, Prem Kumar, a young man working as a sales manager of a multinational cellular phone company, is concerned about it as he is aware of the imminent danger of the use of Internet.

> In the University college campus where I studied, most of the so-called love affairs have turned out to be on contract basis. They were not at all serious. I know this is the case with other colleges too. Now-a-days girls too seem to be more free, flirting and what not. ... They seem to be thinking that if boys can afford such moves and experiences, why can't girls too?
>
> Internet is the main reason for these types of vulgar developments among college youth. Internet is very dangerous. Children too browse pornographic sites, even students studying in Standards 5th and 6th. They do not know even how to browse properly. So café keeps the icons of the 'the wanted sites' in the Desktop. If somebody by chance gets into those sites, he or she feels embarrassed and might show withdrawal tendency. I have come across such cases. Girls too are into it, and they get inspired to move into modelling and fashion shows and loses all their shame and embarrassment in exhibiting them.

With regard to the use of mobile phones, the latest mode of communication, the majority of the respondents seem to look at the utilitarian dimension. Hence, 70.1 per cent (274 respondents) found mobile phone very functional in communication. At the same time, the second largest portion of the sample, (30.2% of the total) regarded the possession of a mobile phone as part of modern lifestyle. Again, we need to explain what they actually mean by 'being modern'. There are also stray opinions that shared the views that mobile phone offers high status and image in the present-day society (8.1%), that it elevates one to the status of high class (3.9%), and that it is undesirable to our culture and ethos (2.5%).

The quantitative analysis of the respondents' opinions on the use of Internet and mobile phones[3] reveal that middle class in general recognizes the fact that the most advanced and sophisticated communication and information channels are part and parcel of the present-day life. A very small percentage of respondents regard that these are also related to status, image and modern lifestyle, or that they are undesirable to our culture and so on. What can be said clearly is that the middle class people on the whole look at the most modern means of communication and information in terms of their function and utility. At the same time, we have some insightful comments on the use of mobile phones, which are indicative of their linkage to the formation of self-image and identity in the age of globalization, wherein the rubrics of consumer culture reign supreme. Samir spoke about the element of glamour and style in possessing a mobile phone, recollecting an interesting incident:

> Once I was walking alone in a busy street. Nearing a *thattu kada* (food and snack sheds on the way side, opened especially at night), I heard a man wearing only an old, shabby bath towel, talking loudly. ... I was not sure to whom he was talking to. ... To my surprise, I realized that he was talking over a mobile. (...) Many advised me to go for a mobile, because it has lots of advantages. ... Many companies come now with new packages. ... So, I am also tempted. ... It has become a real status symbol.

Maya was forthright when she shared her views on possessing cell phones:

> We have a cell phone. But we don't use it now. Actually, there was no need for that. But since it came in the market and was becoming a fashionable item, husband decided to get one. He was mostly using it when he was on tour. If he wanted to inform me about his arrival, especially if he was to get back late, he could conveniently use the mobile, instead of going in search of phone booths. We went for the pre-paid package. Since he had not much use of it, the stipulated money for a given period according to the pre-paid scheme got accumulated and finally he had to make unnecessary calls and finish it off. In a way, so much of money was wasted like that.

And, Seema, in her characteristic style, pointed to the direction in which the use of mobile phones is picking up among middle class:

> Now mobile phone has become a common item. In the beginning, it was not like that. Only a few owned a mobile and it was very expensive too. Now everyone owns mobile phones; no matter what age or occupation. It has become a fashion these days. I don't think all those who own mobiles now are really in need of it; especially students and youth. Surely, for some it comes very handy in their work and profession. Many people are using it just for the sake of using it. It has become a status symbol. Once, our parish priest made an interesting announcement in the church. He announced: "no one should use mobile when they are inside the church for the Service. I know that some are very particular that this instrument must be in their pocket, but they make sure that it is switched off." I have seen many college students possessing mobiles, and more interestingly, college girls keeping it in their vanity bags. For some boys, mobile is an instrument that they are using while travelling in high speed on the motorbike. Those guys think that using a mobile is something great.

Among all the technical factors of mobility, a particular great role is being played by the transport of information – the kind of communication, which does not involve movement of physical bodies, or involves only secondarily and marginally. Technical means were steadily and consistently developed, which allowed information to travel independently from its bodily carriers and also travel from the objects of which the information informed that in a way set the 'signifiers' free from the hold of the 'signified' (Bauman, 1998, p. 15).

> The separation of the movements of information from that of its carriers and its objects allowed in its turn the differentiation of their speed; the movement of information gathered speed on a pace much faster than the travel of bodies, or the change of the situations of which the information informed, was able to reach. In the end, 'the appearance of the computer-served *World Wide Web* that was added to the very notion of 'travel' and of 'distance' to be traveled and rendered information, in

theory as well as in practice, instantaneously available throughout the globe' (ibid).

Following the same line of thought, King looks at the world living in 'super-modernity,' which is the product of global technology and the global play of reflections dependent on the whim of the remote control button (1990, p. 109). He distinguishes between 'place,' which is encrusted with historical moments and social life and 'non-place' where individuals are connected in a uniform manner, and where no organic social life is possible. It is a characteristic of super-modernity that we are in transit through these non-places for more and more of our time. King presents Disney as an example of the fictionality of the world, what he terms 'spectacularizing' and sees non-places having capacity to fictionalise.

Hence, what is important is to examine the nature and dynamics of the effect at the micro level of this 'intensive and extensive forms of cultural flows,' that is rather consensually admitted by social scientists that "it is impossible to be unaffected by it wherever one lives". For many commentators (Sklair, 1991; Sarup, 1996; Beck, 2000), the emergence of global culture is the direct outcome of late capitalist restructuring to shape desires, create needs and, thereby, open up new arenas for capital accumulation. Some view this as an abject surrender to commodification, commercialization and consumerism (Foster, 1985) and blatant cultural degradation by the media, advertising and communication industries in their drive to maximize profits. As Beck comments, contemporary cultural globalization is "a promising route to the profit-paradise" (2000, p. 43). There have been enormous and astonishing social changes in the world on account of the process of globalization. This change is bound up with the emergence of new ways in which we experience space and time. Is there any necessary relation between the emergences of more flexible modes of capital accumulation, new means of 'time-space compression' in the organization of capitalism and in the rise of different cultural forms? Underlying this question is the debate on consumer culture and postmodernity in relation to the question of identity. We explore this aspect of cultural change vis-à-vis postmodern regime in the next concluding chapter.

Notes

1. Popularly known as *bindi* – pattern of colourful mark girls wear on the forehead so as to enhance their beauty and look.
2. The article reports that it would be a difficult choice to make even for the beautician, considering that the market has seen an influx of male commodities. The key players are Baccarose, Park Avenue, Old Spice, Palmolive, Instinct, Jovan, Denim, Nivea, Yardley and Premium. Ten years ago there was just Old Spice. Now you have many choices. See *The Week*, March 30, 1997, pp. 32–42.
3. We do not undertake an examination of the ways in which the introduction of new information and communication technologies (ICTs) have changed communication patterns and relationships and the process of knowledge production. For a detailed study on how Internet has been adopted and its relationship to their international networks, research practices, collaboration, and productivity gender and connectivity initiatives and the impact of the mobile phone on social networking within professional and educational communities, see Miller et al. (2006), Palackal et al. (2007) and Palackal and Shrum (2007).

CHAPTER 8

Shifting Identities

Cultural flows do not just float ethereally across the globe but are always re-inscribed in specific cultural environments. In the purview of globalization, social anthropologists have come to conceptualize culture as being re-inscribed in new time-space contexts, re-localizing it in specific cultural environments, and this process has been familiarly referred to as deterritorialization of culture. To Massey (1994), the issue of deterritorialization of culture is critically linked to the concerns of the cultural economy of globalization, mainly, the organization of the flow of symbols and their sign values.

Majority of respondents, comprising 73.9 per cent of the total, opined that the spectacles that exhibit beauty and body, in fact, conflict with the culture of Kerala. In the same way, 72.2 per cent of the respondents consider that fashion shows, modelling and beauty pageants bring changes in the traditional culture of Kerala. As Table 8.1 shows, the perception remains more or less the same, when the data is analyzed in terms of the variables such as age and sex. This signifies that there is a near unanimity in the middle class belief that the traditional cultural fabric undergoes changes in the wake of consumer culture.

Table 8.1

Age-wise and sex-wise distribution on whether fashion shows or beauty pageants change traditional culture

Sex	*Age group*	*Fashion shows or Beauty pageants change traditional culture*		*Total*
		Yes	*No*	
Male	15–30	73 *(68.9%) 46.5%	33 *(31.1%) 50.0%	106 47.5%
	31–55	72 *(72%) 45.9%	28 *(28%) 42.4%	100 44.8%
	56–70	12 *(70.6%) 7.6%	5 *(29.4%) 7.6%	17 7.6%
	Total	157 100.0%	66 100.0%	223 100.0%
Female	15–30	62 *(78.5%) 60.2%	17 *(21.5%) 50.0%	79 57.7%
	31–55	39 *(71%) 37.9%	16* (29%) 47.1%	55 40.1%
	56–70	2 *(66.7%) 1.9%	1 *(33.3%) 2.9%	3 2.2%
	Total	103 100.0%	34 100.0%	137 100.0%

* Percentage in terms of the respective age group vis-à-vis sex.

Although the middle class in general appear to be great consumers and beneficiaries of the attractive ingredients of consumer culture, generally they position themselves in an accommodative and appropriative mode in the domain of consumer culture. When they really stop to think, they believe that the traditional cultural matrix is negatively affected because of those same attractions and allurements of the consumer culture. It is in the light of this prevailing position on moral ambiguity and negotiation that I explored some areas of social life to unravel the specific effects of cultural shifts in the all pervading purview of consumer culture.

Dance O' Mania

For instance, respondents in general observe that the campus cultural environment in schools, universities and colleges has undergone substantial changes in recent years (Figure 8.1).

Figure 8.1

Opinion on whether items of campus cultural events have changed

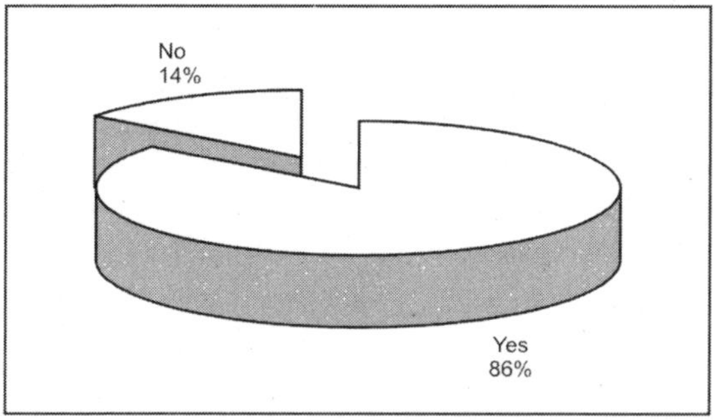

An overwhelming majority of respondents, constituting 85.6 per cent of the total sample, observe that the nature of youth festivals and arts programmes in campuses has undergone considerable changes from earlier days. The change was perceived in terms of the arrival of new items, such as fashion shows, cinematic dance, pop music, beauty pageant etc., which have won predominant currency in students' campus in Kerala. Hence, Seby, a passionate lover of these new varieties of dance and a 'thrill' of the campus, told assertively, "In colleges we have mostly cinematic dance, fusion, fashion shows, beauty pageants, etc. They are called personality contests."

Interestingly, *Vanitha*, the popular women's magazine which is subjected to content analysis, has brought out a special feature on the culture of cinematic dance that has gripped the student campus in Kerala today (January 15–31, 2001, pp. 6–8). It reported that the apparent sentiment of the campus now seems to be that *we are celebrating life* and 'Dance O' Mania' is the buzzword.[1] It also noted that the students are not interested in group dance and folk dance as these are not fashionable. This dance represents the rhythm of the campus and the youth. Students are willing to spend profusely for extensive costumes that are required for cinematic dance. At the same time, some feel that in this wave they also miss certain deep sentiments, imagination and dreams. So, in a nostalgic mood, Maya once reminisced her college days, in the context of our conversation on the contemporary cultural atmosphere of the college campus:

> I find that now-a-days fashion show has become very popular and common in the college campus. In our time, we had *'Kesalankara Malsaram'* (hair style competition) but no fashion shows. Today it has become part and parcel of any college function. During our time, we had meditations and so on for the induction programme. The situation has changed drastically in my Alma Mater too. I heard that last year students began their college day cultural programmes with a fashion show, instead of the invocation dance we traditionally used to have.

Maximum number of respondents seem to think that fashion show (28%) and cinematic dance (26%) are the items, which reign supreme in the cultural stages of college campuses in Kerala. They have also mentioned in the order of priority items like pop music (16.7%), computer animation (11%), beauty pageant (11%) and disco dance (8%). They are found to be the most preferred programmes in the universities, colleges and schools in Kerala. The craze for such programmes has become a real concern for the civil society and polity so much so that the educational department has even banned cinematic dance in the schools and colleges (Figure 8.2).

Figure 8.2

Priority list of new cultural items dominating college campus

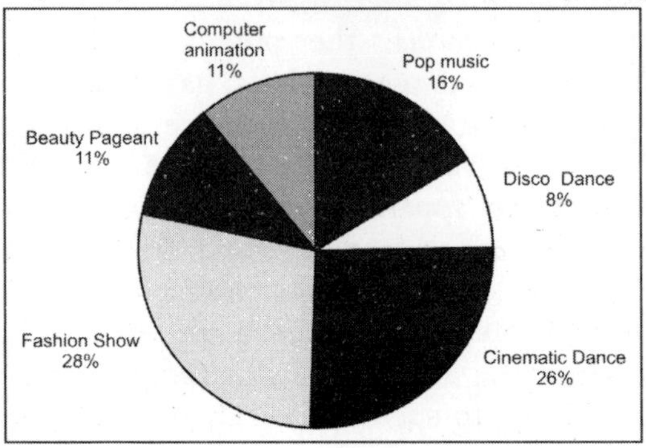

Prem Kumar makes an interesting observation that this process typifies the disposition of the middle class youth in the age of globalization:

> Cinematic dance has no deep values, *Adi Poli* (a recent vernacular expression for something very exciting and interesting) just that. It's just *hai hai* ... But no choice these days than swim along the currents of the day. *Nadodumbum Naduve Odanam* (swim along with the current). I too once joined for a stage programme of cinematic dance for the first time. Anybody can just do it *yaar*. ...

The main reasons stated for the rampant spread of these new kinds of art forms are the influence of television and film. The respondents who shared this perception included 59.7 per cent and 37.2 per cent respectively. A considerable size comprising 35.6 per cent of the respondents believes that the influence of the West also has to be factored as a cause in this regard (Figure 8.3).

Figure 8.3

Reasons for the marked changes in the college campus cultural environment

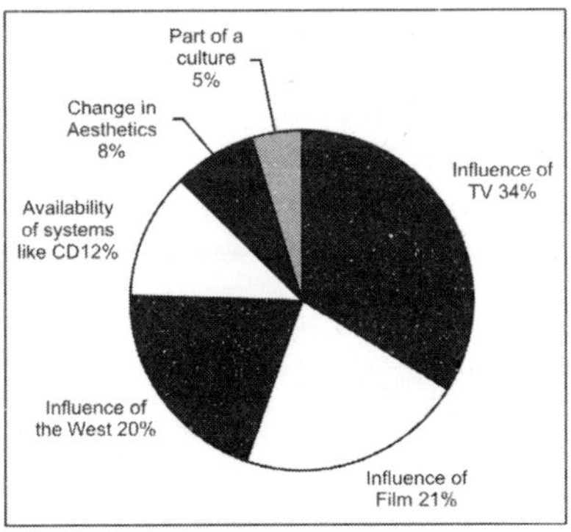

However, Maya was frank in expressing her displeasure of the cinematic dance and such cultural currents rampaging in the campus these days. Maya, in a way, subscribes the general sentiments of middle class itself on the issue:

> Personally, I do not like the new cultural trends and items of the college campus. For instance, some steps of the cinematic

> dance are so vulgar and display a very bad taste. But surprisingly, I find that the main item for any function today is cinematic dance. Everybody appears to be in a frenzy to dance to the music and rhythm of a jumping popular film song and that too played in very high volume. I detest it. But students prefer that to any other item. When I was doing my post graduation, we did not have this at all. The college day celebrations and so on are now full of cinematic dance only.

In fact, it is ironical to note that, along with Maya, the majority of the participants are not in favour of promoting these items that appears to have become integral element of the campus life in these days. A considerable portion of 60 per cent belongs to this category (Figure 8.4).

Figure 8.4

Opinion whether the new cultural items are in tune with consumer culture to be promoted?

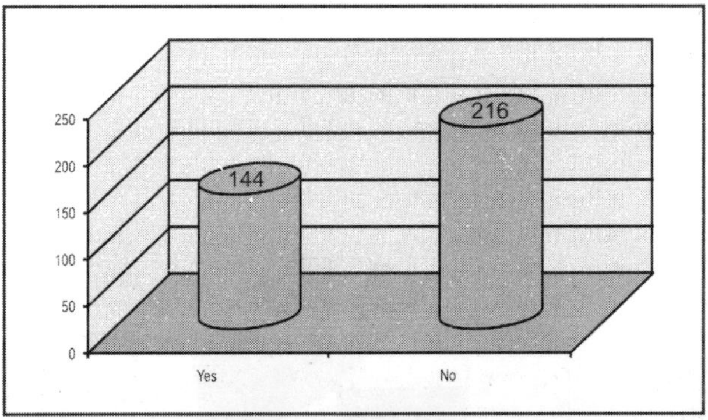

An age-wise distribution of this opinion that does not favour the promotion of the new campus items such as fashion show and cinematic dance reveals that the proportion of the categories makes a downward progression from the youth group to the elderly group. Hence, 54.6 per cent came from the age group 15–30, which constituted 46.8 per cent of the total respondents who supported the idea, whereas a higher percentage of 65.2 belonged to the next age group that comprised the adult category, which provides an equal share of 46.8 per cent to the net portion of the supporters of the idea. However, the elderly who comprised the age group 56–70 had the highest percentage among all the groups, i.e., 70 per cent of their total population, although they had only 6.5 per cent of share in the consolidated percentage, which informed their stance in the matter.

Table 8.2

Age-wise distribution of the respondents who opined whether the new cultural items in the campus are to be promoted

Age group	*Promote new cultural items*		*Total*
	Yes	*No*	
15–30	84 *(45.4%) 58.3%	101 *(54.6%) 46.8%	185 51.4%
31–55	54 *(34.8%) 37.5%	101 *(65.2%) 46.8%	155 43.1%
56–70	6 *(30%) 4.2%	14 *(70%) 6.5%	20 5.6%
Total	144 100.0%	216 100.0%	360 100.0%

* Percentage in terms of the respective age group.

In other words, the maximum number of respondents (i.e., 58.3%) who wish to promote these cultural items hail from the category of youth. Hence, it is the middle class youth who are the prime ambassadors and beneficiaries of these events which are in tune with the currents of consumer culture.

Values in Transition

The cultural atmosphere in the campus in a way exhibits the state of the youth and manifests the attitudinal difference that has gripped their lives in general. Santhosh's sharp comments on the nature of the present-day youth is clearly indicative of this direction:

> Youth have lost their creativity. The present generation seems to be submissive and accommodative unlike the one in the seventies and eighties who were socially more vibrant and, resisting. In those days, we had a creative minority who used to respond to the vital social issues and challenges without being too much worried about the consequences. Now, the

> sentiments of the young people seem to be 'leave us free to hang out in our own world' ... and they are engaged in one's own affair, as though that is the only gateway to be successful. They have become very self-centred and competitive. ...

Adding to Santhosh, Bobby spoke with a tint of reflexivity: "Even in my 'love affair' both of us knew that it is only an adjustment. We were rather sure that it was going to end as we leave the college campus. I must say that 'love' among youth has become very practical... a jolly good time, that's all. This kind of attitude is not part of our culture." Sociological insights prompt us that these marked attitudinal changes in the middle class youth have to be located in the context of the accommodative negotiations in their everyday struggle to forge their identity in a field dominated by the ethics and practices of consumer culture.

Maya recollected her experience as a student counselor pointing to the vital link between identity struggles of the youth vis-à-vis consumer culture:

> Girls get enamoured by certain boys who exhibit lifestyles that are typical of the modern trends. Now it is girls who take such bold initiatives, which was unheard in our times. I had instances of handling many cases while I was working as a counselor in a college in this city.
>
> I still remember the case of a girl who was so taken up by a boy who wore an earring on his left ear and had a long stylish hair. He was good at cinematic dance too. She was after him to be counted as his fiancé. When the boy did not respond to her positively she even went to the extent of cutting her hand and with stains of blood signed his name in a sheet of paper and passed down to him. Later she carved his name in big letters on her forearm with candle wax. The only noticeable quality in that boy was that he was a cinematic dancer and had those modern ways of appearance. The interesting aspect of this episode was that both of them were only pre-degree students.

The phrase "lifestyles that are typical of the modern trends" is to be taken as a special note. As it was unfolded during the course of our empirical expedition, the phrase is to characterize the lifestyle and the efforts of impression management of the middle class in general and the middle class youth in particular, that is demanded in the battlefield of identity construction in an atmosphere heavily charged with consumer culture. With great precision, Reghu Dev captured the dynamics of appropriation, negotiation and the management involved in the business of constructing identities in this cultural scenario. He says:

> It is a question of impression management. ... Everybody tries to project oneself to create an impression and wants to sell better. So, people automatically try to be charming, attractive and impressive. Otherwise today's world renders no identity, recognition or acceptance. The world today gives too much importance to *looking glamorous*. Hence, it is an era of 'impressions.' We need a killer instinct to succeed.
>
> So, youth want to be fashionable and glamorous by all means. All my friends are like that. They want to be part of this modern trend. The thing is that, if one turns away from this trend he/she gets isolated and the most difficult thing for a youth is to get isolated and lonely and so none of us would dare to do that.

The immediate social situation in which 'impression management' efforts take place requires a micro-sociological analysis of interaction. The classical argument in symbolic interactionism, pioneered by Erving Goffman (1959), comes in handy in understanding struggle of the middle class youth in constructing their identity through impression management. Goffman examined the ways in which people understand and seek to influence the perceptions of others through the process of 'impression management'. As social beings, individuals who come into proximity with one another continually look for symbolic indicators of identity and status. They examine and interpret informational cues provided from both the setting and the interaction itself, as if they are actors on a stage using a set, props, and costumes as well as behaviours designed to create certain effects on an audience. An 'impression' given, or given off, is created by both verbal and non-verbal information, accompanied by an interpretation – usually provided by convention or through a script of sorts – through the eyes of co-participants. As each individual is both actor and audience in the drama,[2] the process of information, interpretation, response, and the acquisition of new information is both continuous and mutual. While the number of participants increases, from a dyadic encounter to the campus sites enveloped by consumer culture, the opportunity for multiple stagings also increases.

Now, Prakash extends the changing cultural scenario and the associated shifts in the values in the gamut of consumer culture to the entire purview of society. He opined:

> Societal values in Kerala are losing ground. Social sensitivity has become very low. People have become more individualistic; that whatever happens to the other one is not bothered, even to the point of trampling one's friend to get on with success. Even love and familial bonds have become an adjustment, something to be pursued on contract basis; and so divorce has become rampant; suicide-rates are alarmingly on the increase.

Quantitative investigation almost in ditto subscribed to the perceptions and experience aired in the above narratives. There seems to be near consensus on the view that the nature of relationships in the family has undergone substantial changes compared to that which existed in the preceding decades. Hence, except a negligible proportion of 9.4 per cent, all the respondents are of the opinion that significant changes have occurred in the familial relationships and value system that ruptured the social codes of collective conscious and ethos (Figure 8.5).

Figure 8.5

Whether the nature of relationships in the family changed?

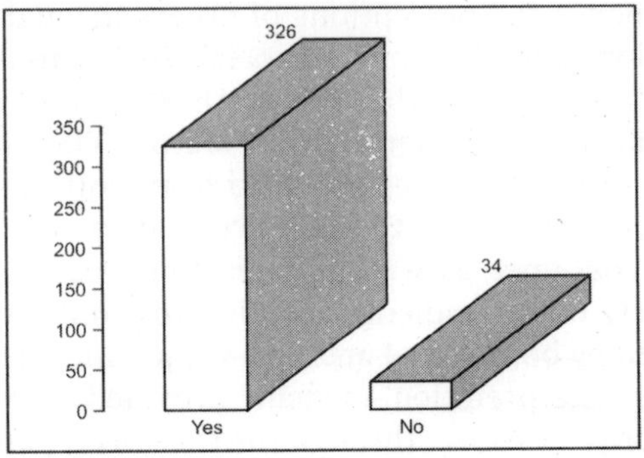

Social-anthropological insights inform us that underlying all manifestations and expressions of culture, there is a system of meanings, of values and criteria, of world views that are translated into languages, gestures, symbols, roles, styles and patterns of life, as well as into the perception, analysis, interpretation and evaluation of reality. In fact, we now precisely tread on the expressions of the non-material aspects (value, attitude and belief) that the contemporary culture ushers in, within the corridors of its corresponding material aspects (technology, commodities and crafts). At this juncture, we argue that in any given society, it is culture that determines and conditions the subjective identity of individuals as well as communities and renders meaning to their relationships, interactions and organizations. In the light of this proposition, we realize the nature of the present-day cultural milieu in which the middle class people who predominate the social demography of this land, move and have their existence.

Table 8.3

Major areas of changes in the family relationship

Changed values	*Yes*	*No*	*NA*
More individualistic	187 (51.9)	140 (38.7)	34 (9.4)
Money-oriented	93 (25.8)	233 (64.7)	34 (9.4)
Utility-based	84 (23.3)	242 (67.2)	34 (9.4)
Elders as burden	107 (29.7)	219 (60.8)	34 (9.4)
Mechanical	93 (25.8)	233 (64.7)	34 (9.4)
Positive change	82.2	318 (88.3)	34 (9.4)

Respondents identified this societal rupture in the following areas in the order of priority. Among them, 51.9 per cent think that Malayalis have become more individualistic in their attitude and approach. Though not in the same proportion, they find that elders are considered as a burden unlike earlier days (29.7%), that life has become more mechanical (25.8%), utility-based (23.3%) and money-minded (25.8%). However, a negligible minority of 2.2% seems to perceive the changes positively.

Identity Shifts

Our discursive exploration has clearly brought to light the element of social construction of identity in the age of globalization. By privileging images, looks, fashion, status and style in the production of identity, post-capitalistic project reinforces the norms of a new consumer culture that offers the possibilities of the production of a different form of "self". The dominant mode of identity kit that the consumer culture confers is neither a rigid code, nor a set of rules to which one must conform, but a field of imagination and creativity in which one can construct any image that one wants. It has also been revealed that the formation of a middle class identity is inextricably linked to striking a pose, vogue, developing an attitude, behaviour and style in a certain way. Therefore, it may be surmised that in the domain of consumer culture, the characteristic feature of contemporary society, identity construction involves one's attitude, values, look, pose and style. In this sense, identity appears to be not deep and essentialist as it was postulated in much of the modern theories, which assumed as the development of an authentic selfhood. For instance, Kellner (1973) noted that for Heidegger, *standing-by-yourself* and *self-constancy* (*Selbstandigkeit*) constituted authentic selfhood and identity.

Media culture in general, and advertising, consumption, fashion and cosmetic industry in particular, constantly destabilize identity and contribute to producing more unstable, fluid, shifting, and changing identities in the contemporary scene. Hence, there are unlimited possibilities in the gamut of all-embracing consumer culture of contemporary society to move from one identity to another, to revel in the play of multiple and plural identities and thus to forge shifting identities.

At the same time, one also observes the inexorable processes of commodification at work in this process of shifting identities. The market segmentation of multiple advertisements campaigns and appeals reproduces and intensifies fragmentation and destabilizes identity, which paradoxically attempts to re-stabilize in conjunction with new products and identifications. The ramifications of consumer culture in many and varied forms of mediascape and related marketing strategies, such as buying habits, consumption styles, practices of taking care of beauty, fashion and appearance, offer a wealth of subject positions, which in turn structure and restructure individual identities. These identities are likely to be multidimensional, polysemic, ideologically coded and open to a variety of readings. Kellner is of the view that these forms of identities are "at the same time expressive of the commodification of culture and demonstrates capitalistic attempts at colonializing the totality of life, from desire to satisfaction" (Kellner, 1995, p. 257).

The problematic of this book was conceived in the backdrop of the debate among social scientists regarding the connection between globalization, consumer culture and postmodernity. Whether contemporary simulated culture and forms of identity should be described as modern or postmodern is still a matter of debate. The findings of this sociological gaze prompt us to argue that it makes more sense to interpret the many facets of the consumer culture and the corresponding forms of identity as emergent postmodern cultural trends. In contrast to the residual traditional values and practices still operative, the cultural scenario that resulted in a hegemonic climate of post-capitalist modernity, commodification, individualism, fragmentation, polysemy, multiplicity and reification are considered as the key constituents of the postmodern age.

In pre-modern societies, identity was unproblematic and not subject to reflection or discussion. An individual is born and died a member of his/her clan – is of a fixed kinship system; and one's tribe or group with one's life trajectory fixed in advance. People did not undergo identity crises, or radically modify their identity. In traditional societies, one's identity was fixed, solid and stable. Identity was a function of predefined social roles and a traditional system of myths which provides orientation and religious sanctions to define one's place in the world, while rigorously circumscribing the realm of thought and behaviour. However, in modernity, identity becomes more mobile, multiple, personal, self-reflective, and subject to change and innovation. Notwithstanding a stable, substantial identity, albeit self-reflexive and freely chosen, was at least a normative goal for the modern self. Hence, the forms of identity in modernity are also relatively substantial and fixed; identity still comes from a circumscribed set of roles and norms – one is a father, a son, a professor, a Malayali, an Indian, a Hindu – a combination of these roles and possibilities. All the same, identities are relatively fixed and limited, though the boundaries of possible identities or of new identities are continually expanding (Kellner, 1995). Yet, identity in modernity is also social and other-related. Theorists of identity from Hegel through Mead have often characterized as personal identity in terms of mutual recognition, as if one's identity depended on recognition from others combined with self-validation of this recognition.

In modernity, identity becomes both a personal and a theoretical problem. Certain tensions appear within and between theories of identity, as well as in modern individuals. On the one hand, some theorists of identity define personal identity in terms of a substantial self, an innate and self-identical essence that constitutes a person. From Descartes' *cogito*, to Kant's and Husserl's transcendental ego, to the enlightenment concept of reason, to some contemporary concepts of the subject at the micro dimension, seems to define identity as constituting the core inner self. For interactionist, identity is conceived as something essential, substantial, unitary, fixed and fundamentally unchanging. Yet other modern theorists of identity postulate a non-substantiality of the self (Hume), or conceive of the self and identity as an existential project, as the creation of the authentic individual (Kierkegaard, Marx, Nietzsche, Heidegger, Sartre). Kellner remarks, "the existential self is always fragile and requires commitment, resolve, and action to sustain, thus making the creation of identity an existential project for each other" (1995, p. 232).

At the same time, modernity also offered new possibilities for constructing personal identities. Modern societies made it possible for individuals to produce, within certain limits, their own identities and to experience identity crisis. Already, in the eighteenth century, the philosopher David Hume formulated the problem of personal identity, of what constituted one's true selfhood, even suggesting that there was no substantial or transcendental self. The issue became an obsession with Rousseau, Kierkegaard, and many other Europeans who experienced rapid social change, the break down of traditional societies and the emergence of modernity.

It is our contention that instead of identity disappearing in contemporary society, it is rather reconstructed and redefined. The experience of the postmodern identity construction is that, it constantly undergoes change and it is integrally linked to the constituents of consumer culture which is defining the mode of contemporary globalization. This postmodern identity tends to be constructed from the images of leisure, consumption, beauty and appearance than modern identities and tends to be more unstable and subject to change. To put it differently, in the postmodern environment of identity formation, it may be more 'natural' to change identities, to switch identities with the changing winds of fashion, impression, appearance and beauty.

While identities of the postmodern period produce an erosion of individuality and social conformity that was typical of modern forms of identity, there are, however, some positive potential built in this postmodern portrayal of identity as an artificial construct. For such a notion of identity suggests that identity can always be reconstructed, that one is free to change and produce oneself as one chooses. In this sense, the postmodern self accepts and affirms multiple and shifting identities. Thus, as Kellner submits: "identity today becomes a freely chosen game, a theatrical presentation of the self, in which one is able to present oneself in a variety of roles, images, and activities, relatively unconcerned about shifts, transformations, and dramatic changes (1995, p. 246).

Therefore, from the postmodern perspective, as the pace, extension and complexity of modern societies accelerate, identity becomes more and more unstable and fragile. In the postmodern culture, the subject has disintegrated into a flux of euphoric intensifiers, fragmented and disconnected, and de-centred and no longer possesses the depth, substantiality, and coherency that was the idea and sometimes achievement of the modern self (Baudrillard, 1983; Jameson, 1983). Postmodern theorists claim that subjects have imploded into masses (Baudrillard, 1983); that a fragmented, disjointed and discontinuous mode of experience is a fundamental characteristic of postmodern culture, at both levels – the level of the subjective experiences and the level of the texts (Jameson, 1983).

In the final analysis, it is submitted that it is more appropriate to consider multiple and unstable identities as characterizing the contemporary cultural milieu than were the case previously. Modern identities – however multiple and subject to change – appeared to be more stable whereas there currently seems to be more acceptance of change, fragmentation, and theatrical play with identity than was the case in the earlier epoch of modernity. On the one hand, this increases one's freedom to play with one's identity and to dramatically change one's life, while on the other hand it can lead to a totally fragmented, disjointed life, subject to the whims of predicaments offered by the subtle indoctrinations of consumer culture. Against totally dispersed, fragmented and disconnected identity, one might want to valorize certain features central to modern identity, like autonomy, rationality, commitment, responsibility, and so on or one might want to reconstruct these concepts. In any case, identity continues to be a problematic, though it has been problematized anew in the current orgy of commodification, fragmentation, image production, and societal, political and cultural transformation that is the work of consumer capitalism.

Cultural Domination

The advantage of this shift in the constitution of identity is that it suggests that one can change, that one can remake oneself, that one can free oneself from whatever traps and restrictions one finds oneself encased in. The disadvantage is that identity becomes flattened out and trivialized in terms of style, look, and consumption in which one is defined by one's image, possessions and lifestyle. One's identity is a construct, constituted out of the material of one's life situation; one can change and transform one's life according to one's projects, as Sartre, Foucault and others remind us. But constituting a substantial identity requires will, action, commitment, intelligence and creativity. Notwithstanding, many of the postmodern identities constructed out of consumer culture lack these features; being little more than a game someone plays, a pose, a style and look that one can dispose of tomorrow for a new look and image – in a way, disposable and easily replaceable identities for the postmodern carnival.

In the context of this pervading social process, it seems possible to speak of an identifiable 'global culture' as actually existing. Among the most obvious and tangible forms, cultural globalization is the products of the Western media although the reception as well as impact of these cultural goods are hard to gauge. For instance, television opened the macro-scope with its capacity for instantaneous transmission via satellite for global icons like Michael Jackson and Madonna, the global proliferation of products like Coca-Cola and McDonald's and a wide range of Western consumer goods. It is in this context of the spread of western forms of cultural materials that Appadurai talks about cultural homogenization:

> The globalization of culture is not the same as its homogenization, but globalization involves the use of a variety of instruments of homogenization (armaments, advertising techniques, language hegemonies and clothing styles) that are absorbed into local, political and cultural economies, only to be repatriated as heterogeneous dialogues of national sovereignty, free enterprise and fundamentalism in which the state plays an increasingly delicate role (1996b, p. 57).

Global culture is not something similar to national cultures. In his view, there are as yet no global equivalences to the ethnic cores composed of a patchwork of competing national myths, legends, memories, stories, symbols, events and heroes, etc., sedimented within national consciousness and which give identity to a nation and its people. In comparison, global culture is held to be mainly a recent media-driven construct. Local and national cultures have strong emotional connotations for large numbers of people, but global culture is bereft of such 'ethnic-based' appeal. While global culture can certainly draw upon folk and national cultures, it is not based on shared global stories and memories. In this regard, Perry (1998) opines that it is 'memory-less', syncretistic of and dependent upon the profit-seeking production of mass-mediated signs and symbols. Whereas local culture is closely tied to place and time, global culture is free from these constraints: as such it is 'disconnected', 'disembedded' and 'de-territorialized', existing outside the usual reference to geographical territory (Featherstone, 1990, 1995).

Robertson argues that global culture is "just meaningful as the idea of national and local culture" (1992, p. 114). More than before, we witness the interpenetration of cultures as nations come under intense pressure to connect what he terms 'inwardness and outwardness'. Some others point to global culture's diverse character and to the fact that because of its technologized nature, it does not resemble to anything that has previously moved around the world. So, Hannerez believes that the net result of the movement of this global culture can be described as,

> no longer so easy to conform to the ideal type of a locale,' given the '... influx of meanings as well as of people and goods ... the inter-connectedness of various local cultures ... the development of cultures without a clear anchorage in any one territory ... and a global, inter-connected diversity (1990, p. 237).

Therefore, the contemporary cultural globalization is generally seen in the social science parlance as different from anything that has superseded, in that, for the first time ever, it is impossible to be unaffected by it wherever one lives. Held et al., (1999) conclude:

> [...] there is no historical equivalent of the global reach and volume of cultural traffic through contemporary telecommunication, broadcasting and transport infrastructures [...] (p. 327) [...] no historical parallel exists for such intensive and extensive forms of cultural flows (p. 368).

In the contemporary cultural scenario, different categories of people embark upon varied political and cultural representations by way of responsive assertions, as they confront the unique market behaviour triggered of in the wake of globalization. These responsive assertions often assume different forms and manifestations apparently on opposite and contradictory terms. The two major contrasting modes of such assertive mobilizations found in the Indian polity today are: (1) the revamping of the micro organic strength of the primordial elements, familiarly known as 'identity politics' on the one side, and (2) the political mobilizations of nationalist agenda on communal and fundamentalist ties along the fascist tendencies on the other side. In the context of the weakening of nation-state politics and the waning of secular bonding, these collective assertions may be viewed as everyday struggles to create a cultural space and subjectivity in the face of an experience of a ruptured self and identity that is induced on account of the popular culture generated by globalization.

The Road Ahead

This sociological gaze embarked upon an expedition on the aspect of contradiction and ambiguities in the lives of the middle classes at the micro level with regard to the values and the practice as they engage with globalization. In a sense, it opened up a line of enquiry into the plight of 'the divided subjects' in the social and cultural aspects of human's lives in contemporary society. A deeper investigation into the macro dimension of this aspect of moral ambiguity and negotiations will hopefully highlight the roots of the ambiguities and negotiations in contemporary societal reality as well as in their collective manifestations.

The present study brought to surface the fact that how consumer culture has made it possible for the increasing visibility of the body – in both popular culture and the media – through sexed representation and body-transformative practices. This has caught the focus of academic debate. A further analysis on the questions on the social construction and disciplining of women's bodies and gender positions in the light of the 'beauty lust and the cult of the body' that is insidiously pervasive in contemporary Kerala society will further illumine the debates in contemporary feminist theory. Along with this, the present-day experience of alienation and atomization of individuals and the rampant tendencies of depression, divorce and suicide could be brought to further scrutiny.

The significance of power relations in the ambit of globalization will be another area of further investigation. Given the socio-economic and political conditions in the wake of globalization in a region like Kerala, people are pulled into different directions – by their own thoughts and values and powers of those around. In this context, a study on the cultural processes that form part of the world of unequal social and economic power relations within the family and within the wider society will be relevant. The role of the global marketplace developed in the wake of globalization in transforming the parameters of the development has been an important theme of debate in recent developmental discourse. The economic and fiscal policies and social welfare measures have been renewed on a global scale based on this shift in the market principle. Likewise, the techno-cultural spheres too have undergone changes and their magnitude has spread across regions and nations criss-crossing political boundaries. It has been argued that this globalization process shatters the old definition of development as nationally organized economic growth. This situation gives rise to a developmental discourse in India, which is bedeviled by the debate between self-reliance and globalization. In this context, a further study on the dynamics of this paradigm shift from modernization to the project of developmentalism in the contemporary socio-political backdrop of the efforts in people's planning and Panchayati Raj, is worth pursuing. Related to this is the study on the impact of global economy on the Indian agro-cultural life, especially in the wake of the alarming magnitude of the suicide cases being reported in many agricultural settings in India.

Notes

1. Incidentally, 'Dance O' Mania' was the main caption of the School Fest organized by a prestigious school in the capital city of Kerala in 2006.
2. This school is called 'dramaturgy' or the 'dramaturgical perspective' for this reason.

Bibliography

Adorno, T. (1984). *Aesthetic Theory*. London, Routledge and Kegan Paul.

Appadurai, A. (1986). "Introduction: Commodities and the Politics of Value". *The Social Life of Things*. A. Appadurai. Cambridge, Cambridge University Press.

——. (1991). *Global Ethnoscapes: Notes and Queries for a Transnational Anthropology. Recapturing Anthropology*. N.M. School of American Research Press.

——. (1996a). *Modernity at Large-Cultural Dimensions of Globalisation*. Minneapolis, University of Minnesota Press.

——. (1996b). "Playing with Modernity". *Consuming Modernity: Public Culture in Contemporary India*. (ed.) C.A. Breckenridge. Delhi, Oxford University Press.

——. (1999). "Globalisation and the Research Imagination." *International Social Science Journal* (160): 231–238.

Ang, I. (1985). *Watching Dallas: Soap Opera and the Melodramatic Imagination*. London, Methuen.

——. (1990). "Culture and Communication." *European Journal of Communication*, 5(2–3): 239–260.

——. (1996). *Living Room Wars*. London, Routledge.

Bandhu, P. (2001). *Dancing To Global Capital: Media in India*. Chennai, Vikas Adhyan Kendra.

Bardhan, P. (1984). *The Political Economy of Development in India*. Delhi, OUP.

Barker, C. (1997). *Global Television*. Oxford and Cambridge, Blackwell.

Barthes, R. (1972 [1957]). *Mythologies*. London, Paladin.

Baudrillard, J. (1975). *The Mirror of Production*. St Louis, Telos Press.

——. (1981). *For a Critique of the Political Economy of the Sign*. St Louis, Telos Press.

——. (1983). *Simulations*. New York, Semiotext (e).

——. (1988). *Selected Writings*, (ed.) Mark Poster. Stanford, Stanford University.

Bauman, Z. (1991). *Modernity and Ambivalence*. Cambridge, Polity Press.

——. (1998). *Globalization: The Human Consequences*. Cambridge, Polity Press.

Baxi, U. and Parekh, B. (1995). *Crisis and Change in Contemporary India*. New Delhi, Sage.

Beck, U. (2000). *What is Globalization*. Polity Press, Cambridge.

Berger, P. (1963). *Invitation to Sociology*. New York, Doubleday.

Bhatia, B.M. (1994). *India's Middle Class*. Delhi, Konark Publishers.

Cohen, A.P. (1994). *Self Consciousness: An Alternative Anthropology of Identity*. London, Routledge.

Cole, G.D.H. (1950). "The Conception of the Middle Class." *British Journal of Sociology*, Vol. 1.

Craik, J. (1994). *The Face of Fashion: Cultural Studies in Fashion*. London, Routledge.

Cvetkovich, A. and Kellner, D. (1997). (eds) *Articulating the Global and the Local*. Boulder, Colorado, US, Westview Press.

Dreze, J. and Sen, A. (2002). *India Development and Participation*. New Delhi, Oxford University Press.

Featherstone, M. (1990). *Global Culture: Nationalism, Globalization and Modernity*. London, Sage

——. (1991). *Consumer Culture and Postmodernism*. London, Sage.

——. (1992). "Postmodernism and the Aestheticisation of Everyday Life". *Modernity and Identity*. (eds) Lash, Scott and Jonathan. Friedman, Oxford and Cambridge, Blackwell

——. (1995). *Undoing Culture: Globalization, Postmodernism and Identity*. London, Sage.

Foucault, M. (1977). *Discipline and Punish*. Harmondsworth, Penguin.

Friedman, J. (1997). "Global crises, the struggle for cultural identity and intellectual Pork Barrelling: cosmopolitans versus locals, ethnics and nationals in an era of de-hegemonisation". *Debating*

Cultural Hybridity. (eds) Pnina Werbner and T. Modood. London, Zed Books.

——. (2002). "Globalisation and Localization". *The Anthropology of Globalisation*. Jonathan Xavier and Renato Rosaldo, Massachusetts, Oxford, Blackwell.

George, K.K. (1993). *Limits to Kerala Model of Development: An analysis of fiscal crisis and its implications*. Thiruvananthapuram, Centre for Development Studies.

Giddens, A. (1990). *The Consequences of Modernity*. Cambridge, Polity Press.

——. (1991). *Modernity and Self-Identity: Self and Society in the Late Modern Age*. Cambridge, Polity Press.

Goffman, E. (1959). *The Presentation of Self in Everyday Life*. New York, Anchor.

Gulati, L. (1992). *Economic and Social Aspects of Population Aging in Kerala, India*. New York, Department of Economic and Social Development, United Nations.

Gupta, A. and James Ferguson (1997). *Culture, Power, Place: Excavation in Critical Anthropology*. Durham, Duke University Press.

Gupta, Dipankar (2000). *Mistaken Identity: India Between Worlds*. New Delhi, Harper Collins.

Hall, S. (1992). *The Question of Cultural Identity. Modernity and its Futures*. S. Hall, Held, D. and McGrew. Cambridge, Polity Press.

Hannerez, U. (1990). "Cosmopolitans and locals in world culture". *Global Culture*. (ed.) M. Featherstone. London, Sage.

——. (1992). *Cultural Complexity: Studies in the Social Organization of Meaning*. New York, Columbia University Press.

Harvey, D. (1989). *The Condition of Postmodernity: An Enquiry into the Origins of Cultural Change*. Oxford, Basil Blackwell.

Haug, Wolfgang (1986). *Critique of Commodity Aesthetics*. Cambridge, Polity Press.

——. (1987). *Commodity Aesthetics, Ideology and Culture*. New York, International General.

Hebdige, D. (1979). *Subculture: The Meaning of Style*. New York, Methuen.

——. (1989). "After the Masses". *New Times: The Changing Face of Politics in the 1990s*. (eds) S. Hall, and Jacques, M., London, Lawrence and Wishart.

——. (1990). *Cut 'N' Mix: Culture, Identity and Caribbean Music*. New York, Routledge.

Held, D. (1995). *Democracy and the Global Order*. Cambridge, Polity.

Held, D. et al. (1999). *Global Transformations: Politics, Economics and Culture*. Cambridge, Polity Press.

Inda, X. J. and Rosaldo, R. (2002). "Introduction: A World in Motion". *The Anthropology of Globalisation: A Reader*. (eds) J. X. and Renato, Rosaldo. Massachusetts and Oxford, Blackwell Publishers: 1–35.

Irigaray, L. (1985). *This Sex Which Is Not One*. Ithaca, Cornell University Press.

James, J. (1993). *Consumption and Development*. New York, Martins Press.

Jameson, F. (1983). "Postmodernism, and the consumer society". *Postmodern Culture*. (ed.) H. Foster. Seattle, Bay View.

——. (1984). "Postmodernism, or the Cultural Logic of Late Capitalism." *New Left Review*, 146.

Kellner, D. (1973). *Heidegger's Concept of Authenticity*. Columbia University, University Reprint Service.

——. (1995). *Media Culture: Cultural studies, Identity and Politics between the Modern and the Post-modern*. London, Routledge.

Kemper, S. (1993). "The Nation Consumed – Buying and Believing in Sri Lanka." *Public Culture*, Vol. 5(No. 3): 377–393.

King, A.D. (1990). *Global Cities*. London, Routledge.

Kohli, A. (1991). *Democracy and Discontent: India's Growing Crisis of Governability*. Cambridge, Cambridge University Press.

Kothari, R. (1989). *Politics and the People*. Delhi, Ajanta.

Krishnan, P. and Anita Dighe (1990). *Affirmation and Denial: Construction of Femininity on Indian Television*. New Delhi, Sage.

Kroker, A. and Cook, D. (1986). *The Postmodern Scene*. Chicago, University of Chicago Press.

Kumar, K. (1994). "Battle Against their own Minds: Notes on Literate Kerala." *Economic and Political Weekly*, Vol. XXIX (No. 7): 345–347.

Kulkarni, V. G. (1992). "The Middle Class Bulge." *Far Eastern Economic Review* January 14.

Laclau, E. and Mouffe, C. (1985). *Hegemony and Socialist Strategy, Towards A Radical Democratic Politics*. London, Verso.

Lash, S. and Urry, J. (1994). *The End of Organized Capitalism*. Cambridge, Polity Press.

Lefebvre, H. (1971). *Everyday Life in the Modern World*. London, Allen Lane.

Lett, D.P. (1998). *In Pursuit of Status: The Making of South Korea's "New" Urban Middle Class*. Cambridge, London, Harvard University Asia Centre.

Liebes, T. and E. Katz (1990). *The Export of Meaning: Cross-cultural Readings of Dallas.* New York, Oxford.

Lull J. and Hinerman S. (1997). *Media Scandals: morality and desire in the popular culture marketplace.* Cambridge, Polity Press.

Luke, T.W. (1995). "New world order or neo-world orders". *Global Modernities.* (eds) M. Featherstone, Lash, S. and Robertson, R. London, Sage.

Mankekar, P. (1999). *Screening Culture, Viewing Politics: An Ethnography of Television, Womanhood, and Nation in Postcolonial India.* Durham and London, Duke University Press.

Marshall, G., Ed. (1994, second edition 1998). *A Dictionary of Sociology.* New York, Oxford University Press.

Massey, D. (1994). *Space, Place and Gender.* Cambridge, Polity.

McMichael, P. (1996). "Globalization: Myths and Realities." *Rural Sociology* Vol. 61(No. 1): 25–55.

Mead, G.H. (1934/1962). *Mind, Self and Society: From the Standpoint of a Social Behaviorist.* Chicago, University of Chicago Press.

Michaels, E. (2002). "Hollywood Iconography: A Warlpiri Reading". *The Anthropology of Globalization.* (ed.) R. Rosaldo. Massachusetts, Oxford, Blackwell: 311–324.

Miller, D. (1995). "Consumption as the Vanguard of History: A Polemic by Way of an Introduction". *In Acknowledging Consumption.* D. Miller. London, Routledge.

Mills, C.W. (1951). *White Collar: The American Middle Class.* New York, Oxford University Press.

Mooji, D.M. (1998). *Global Marketing and Advertising: Understanding Cultural Paradoxes.* London, Sage.

Morley, D. and Kevin Robins (1995). *Spaces and Identity: Global Media, Electronic Landscapes, and Cultural Boundaries.* London, Routledge.

Nair, R. (1974). *Middle Class in Kerala.* Trivandrum, The Kerala Academy of Political Science.

Nandy, A. (1990). "The Politics of Secularism and the Rediscovery of Religious Tolerance". *Mirrors of Violence, Communities, Riots and Survivors in South Asia.* V. Das. Delhi, Oxford University Press

Oommen, M.A. (1992). *The Kerala Economy.* New Delhi, Oxford and IBH.

Oommen, M.A., ed. (1999). *Kerala's Development Experience,* Vol. 1 and 11. New Delhi, Concept Publishing.

Perry, N. (1998). *Hyper-Reality and Global Culture.* London, Routledge.

Poster, M. (1988). (ed.)*Selected Works of Jean Baudrillard.* Polity Press, Cambridge.

Ramachandran, V. K. (1996). "On Kerala's Development Achievements". *Indian Development: Selected Regional Perspectives.* (eds) J. Dreze. and A. Sen. Delhi, Oxford University Press: 205–356.

Robertson, R. (1992). *Globalization: Social Theory and Global Culture.* London, Sage.

Saberwal, S. (1996). *Roots of Crisis: Interpreting Contemporary Indian Society.* Delhi, Sage.

Sarup, M. (1996). *Identity, Culture and the Postmodern World.* Edinburgh, Edinburgh University Press.

Saussure, F.D. (1966). *Course in General Linguistics.* New York, McGraw Hill.

Schiller, H. (1976). *Communication and Cultural domination.* White Plains, N.Y, International Arts and Sciences.

——. (1985). *Electronic Information Flows as the New Basis for Global Domination. Television in Transition.* Drummond, R. London, BFI.

——. (1996). *Information Inequality.* London, Routledge.

Simon, W. (1996). *Postmodern Sexualities.* London, Routledge.

Singh, G. (1985). *The New Middle Class in India.* Jaipur, Rawat Publications.

Smith, A.D. (1990). "Towards a Global Culture." *Theory, Culture and Society,* Vol. 7.

Spybey, T. (1996). *Globalisation and World Society.* Cambridge, Polity Press.

Tanter and Young (1990). *The Politics of Middle Class Indonesia.* Clayton, Victoria, Australia, Monash University.

Therborn, G. (1995). "Routes to/through Modernity'. *Global Modernities.* M. Featherstone, Lash, S. and Robertson, R. London, Sage.

Thompson, J.B. (1995). *The Media and Modernity: A Social Theory of the Media.* Stanford, Stanford University Press.

Thompson, K. (1992). *Social Pluralism and Postmodernity. Modernity and its Futures.* Cambridge, Polity Press.

Tomlison, J. (1991). *Cultural Imperialism.* Baltimore, Johns Hopkins University Press.

——. (1999). *Globalisation and Culture.* Cambridge and Oxford, Polity and Blackwell.

Van Der Veer, P. (1994). *Religious Nationalism: Hindus and Muslims in India.* Berkeley, University of California Press.

Varma, P.K. (1998). *The Great Indian Middle Class.* New Delhi, Viking, Penguin Books.

Veblen, T. (1899). *The Theory of the Leisure Class.* New York, New American Library of World Literature Inc.

Vera-Toscano and Chapman, P. (1999). *Global Changes and Individual Responses in Rural Areas – The Dynamics of Low Income and Household Economic Status. Local Responses to Global Integration.* Papadopoulos. Aldershot, Ashgate.

Vogel, E.F. (1963). *Japan's New Middle Class: The Salary Man and His Family.* London, University of California Press.

Waters, M. (1995). *Globalization.* London and New York, Routledge.

Wessel, M.V. (2001). *Modernity and Identity: An Ethnography of Moral Ambiguity and Negotiations in an Indian Middle Class.* Amsterdam, University of Amsterdam.

Willis, P. (1977). *Learning to Labour.* Farnborough, Saxon House.

Index